LIFE AND WORKS OF

PHILLIS WHEATLEY

PHILLIS WHEATLEY

LIFE AND WORKS OF

PHILLIS WHEATLEY

CONTAINING HER COMPLETE POETICAL WORKS.
NUMEROUS LETTERS, AND A COMPLETE
BIOGRAPHY OF THIS FAMOUS
POET OF A CENTURY AND
A HALF AGO.

— BY —

G. HERBERT RENFRO.

ALSO A SKETCH OF THE LIFE OF MR. RENFRO

BY

LEILA AMOS PENDLETON.

WASHINGTON, D. C.
1916

Reprinted by Mnemosyne Publishing Co., Inc. Miami, Florida

PUBLISHED BY
ROBERT L. PENDLETON, 1216 YOU STREET
WASHINGTON, D. C.

First Mnemosyne reprinting 1969

**Reprinted from a copy in the
Fisk University Library Negro Collection.**

Copyright © 1969   Mnemosyne Publishing Co., Inc.   Miami, Florida

Library of Congress Catalog Card Number:
70-83899

Printed in the United States of America

GLOSTER HERBERT RENFRO.

GLOSTER HERBERT RENFRO, the second son of George
W. and Mary E. Renfro, was born November 25th, 1867,
at Washington, D. C. He died February 10th, 1894, in
the prime of early manhood, not, however, without having
made his mark upon his day and generation. The story of his
life should serve as inspiration and incentive to every youth of
the Negro race. At an age when most young persons are oc-
cupied with trying to get the most pleasure out of life, the
heart of Herbert Renfro was filled with love and pity for his
race and his mind was bent upon acquiring a sound education,
that he might worthily do his share toward their uplift.
This lofty aim became an integral part of his life by inheri-
tance as well as training, for his parents were deeply im-
bued with race feeling. They were content to suffer loss
pecuniary, and otherwise, if thereby they might help forward race development.

After a course in the local public schools, young Renfro at
the age of 14, entered the Preparatory Department of Howard
University, where his studious habits and gentlemanly deportment won for him the high regard of both teachers and fellow-
students. At seventeen years of age he entered the College
Department and took the lead in his classes, showing himself
especially proficient in mathematics and the classics. The
death of his father, however, forced him to leave college after
having completed the sophomore term.

For a while he taught school in Maryland, his work there
measuring up to the highest standards, but in April, 1888, he
was appointed to a position as clerk in the Post Offie at Washington, D. C., and in October of the same year he entered upon a
course in the Law Department of Howard University. Here,
too, he made his mark and attracted especial attention to himself by his easy mastery of his subjects.

On May 26, 1890, Mr. Renfro received the degree of LL. B.,
and, having been unanimously elected to that honor, deliv-
ered the valedictory address of his class in such a manner as to

make a great impression upon his audience. Two months later he was admitted to the bar of the District of Columbia and from that time until his health failed, he practiced his profession creditably and with notable success.

Perhaps the most striking quality of his character was his unswerving loyalty ; he invariably supported race enterprises regardless of personal advantage ; he took the greatest pride in the history of our past and he had unbounded admiration for the noble and talented individuals who have sprung from Negro stock. As will have been gathered, his love for literature was great and that he, himself, was a writer of no mean ability the appended sketch of the life of Phillis Wheatley, as well as many other articles from time to time contributed to newspapers and magazines will show.

Today there seems to be entering into the race-life of the Negro a Renaissance, the outward evidences of which are the putting into more general practice those principles which animated Gloster Herbert Renfro.

We may well believe that the spirit of this young man, together with all others who were like-minded, yet watches over his beloved people and hails with joy the dawning of the New Day.

LEILA AMOS PENDLETON.

Washington, D. C.,
September 5th, 1916.

CONTENTS

PHILLIS WHEATLEY

SKETCH OF

THE LIFE OF PHILLIS WHEATLEY.

BY G. HERBERT RENFRO.

ONE century ago American literature, then in its infancy, received no small degree of enrichment from the poetic genius of an African slave. PHILLIS WHEATLEY was born in what is generally termed the"Dark Continent," on the western coast of Africa, about the year 1753 or '54. There is no definite means of ascertaining to what particular tribe she belonged. Suffice it to say that she was born in, and transported from, that particular section of Africa in which the enemies of the Negro race have discovered the lowest grade of human intellect. Her birthplace, like that of her great predecessor, whom cultured Rome was pleased to applaud, is a monument sacred to the African alone, and an honor for which a tribe or kingdom might proudly contend.

Our subject was stolen from her home and parents in her baby years by cruel men, who decreed for her perpetual slavery. She was about seven years of age when dragged from the land of her fathers by those who professed to be civilized Christian men. Those cold hearts packed away this babe in company with seventy or eighty other girls (many of the same age, tenderness and innocence)—in a slave ship of less than ordinary comfort. The quarters are described as having been a room thirteen by twenty-five feet, and five feet eight inches high. After a sickening voyage across the stormy Atlantic, a landing was made in the Boston harbor, whereupon the girls were transferred to a building as unhealthy and repulsive as the hold of the ship, and a few days later were exposed for sale in a market house. This occurred in the year 1761.

Boston, the eye of America, the modern intellectual Athens, is one of the freest cities of the world to-day, yet one hundred years ago it was a common thing to visit the markets and purchase children. Amid a host of others, a little, nameless, homeless, friendless babe was at that time offered for sale; sick and fatigued from the long journey across the sea, from bad food and harsh treatment, with bare head and bare feet, with a short, dirty piece of carpet as her only clothing and protection in that chilly clime. Who was her father? Perhaps his body lay dead and exposed to the wild beasts on African soil, where he had fallen in defense of home and family, country and liberty. Had she a mother? Thousands of miles and a deep ocean lay between them. Though Phillis was seven years of age, her recollection of past events in her life, or other peculiarities of her native land, was very slight. It is a matter of impossibility to discover at what period of her life the parents were bereft of their child, how long she was in captivity or slavery before leaving the shores of Africa, how she fared and spent her time, and other things of which we regret that no information can be obtained. The only distinct impression that remained upon the infant mind was that every morning her mother was accustomed to "pour out water before the rising sun," perhaps in the expression of reverence in the recognition of a Supreme and Almighty Being.

The slave-market of Boston, on this occasion, was crowded with slaves and purchasers. Among the latter, passing and re-passing, Mrs. Wheatley, the wife of John Wheatley, a tailor, residing in King Street (now known as State Street), became pleased with the intelligent face, modest demeanor and gentle appearance of the little waif, at once struck a bargain, paid her price in gold, and conducted her newly-acquired property to her home. Here the child was supplied with decent clothing, wholesome food and comfortable lodging, and even more than this—with a name. The generous hand of Providence found the sweet-sounding name of Phillis Wheatley.

At this time the Wheatley family consisted of John Wheatley, his wife Susannah, and their twin children, Nathaniel and Mary. There were also several Negro slaves attached to the household who had grown old in service. Mrs. Wheatley's purpose in purchasing a child of this tender age (for Phillis was adjudged to be seven or eight years, from the circumstance of shedding her front teeth) appears to have been a provision for her own future—a design to obtain a young girl who could be trained under her own eye as a faithful domestic for her approaching old age. Young Phillis was even then of slender frame and delicate constitution. Doubtless her mistress, who was yet to display an unusual benevolence, would never have exacted from her very arduous burdens. Nature had designed Phillis for a queen, not for a slave.

The daughter, Mary Wheatley, then about eighteen years of age, took charge of Phillis, and began to instruct the child in the ordinary household duties, as well as in the English tongue. Though unable to speak a word of the English language when first placed in her hands, Miss Wheatley soon discovered a remarkable brightness and eagerness in her new pupil. So apt was the young slave, just eight years of age, in acquiring learning and remembering, that Mrs. Wheatley had no heart to check the rising genius or damp the intellectual ardor of the child. But on the other hand, far different from many familiar tales, contrary to the spirit of ignorance on which slavery subsists, this generous mistress extended the means and opportunities of instruction, and permitted her daughter to teach the alphabet to the slave. So rapid was the progress made that, sixteen months later, the most difficult portions of the Bible were read with ease and fluency by the little African.

Having learned to read, Phillis readily learned to write, her own curiosity prompting to it, as her master testified. Possessing at first no writing materials, her genius improvised some for the occasion. Not being supplied with pen and paper, she found ever-ready substitutes in a piece of chalk or charcoal and brick wall. In this and other ways indicating unusual ability, much attention was directed to her from the Wheatley household. That excellent family soon learned that, instead of obtaining a spirit born to serve, there had come among them a spirit born to create. In her twelfth year Phillis was able to carry on an extensive correspondence on the most important and interesting topics of the day with many of the wisest and most learned in Boston and London. Having mastered the

English language within the short period of four years she began the study of the Latin tongue, and her progress in this was
only paralleled by her remarkable record in the study of English. She soon made a translation of one of Ovid's tales. It
was considered so admirable for one so young, and so extraordinary for one of the African race, that friends insisted upon
its publication. The translation was received with great favor,
and on her visit to England, a few years later, it was repub-
lished, calling forth many encomiums from the public press.

The news of such progress, made even in the large city of
Boston by an unknown African slave, could not be concealed.
Public attention was directed toward her. Friends of the
Wheatleys, refined and intelligent, came to visit the Africa
prodigy, to witness her proficiency, and to cultivate her
friendship. Thus becoming acquainted with many of the best
people of Boston, she was often invited to their homes, and,
during these visits, mindful of the prejudice against her race,
she always conducted herself in so becoming a manner, while
a recipient of honors, as to give no offense to the most pre-
judiced mind whom accident or design might cause her to
meet on these occasions.

The city of Boston was even then the intellectual metropolis
of the New World, having within her confines a numerous
class of men distinguished for their literary attainments. Yet,
education was not so widely disseminated as to be regarded as
universal. The illiteracy of the master was often covered by
the pride of his station, but that of the slave was exposed to
the sunlight. Hence, we can account in a measure for the indulgence shown to Phillis, and the curiosity excited by her
efforts. Here was a slave girl, just entering upon her teens,
whose entire education was gathered from private instruction
of a few years at her master's house, who was able to converse and
discuss with the most learned and cultivated people of Boston;
many of whom sought her society, loaned her books, gave her
encouragement, acknowledged her merit and respected her
abilities. Nor is this the first occasion in history that the wise
and intelligent have found worth and merit in the conversation and virtues of a child.

When, at the age of ten years, the leading poetess of the

world, Elizabeth Barrett, began to compose, her precocious talent was greeted with unbounded commendations, while every advantage of education, refinement and culture was showered upon her. She was not merely sprinkled with the occasional drops of literary wisdom, but thoroughly immersed in its deepest waters. She was decked with gems from every storehouse of knowledge, and yielded every light from the literary world. But the instruction to Phillis was rudimental and fragmentary. Far be it from us to render any impression other than the kindest appreciation for the education and instruction extended by Mrs. Wheatley to this slave girl; far be it from us to cast anything but praise and commendation for the benevolence and interest in young Phillis, and more, the motherly affection and encouragement to this friendless genius; but in the name of humanity which makes us detest the master and pity the slave, no matter how favorable the conditions and circumstances of the servitude; in the name of justice, which makes us believe that all men are brothers, free and equal in brth; in the name of truth, which compels us to say that Phillis served as slave and was recognized as property for a number of years—it was utterly impossible that her talents could be fully developed, or that she could enjoy more than a small share of the advantages common to the freer and lighter-hued daughters of the land.

After the translation of Ovid's poem had been published, Phillis devoted herself assiduously to the muses and cultivated a natural taste for poetry. In the very first year of her education her progressive and intellectual spirit had been observed, while the tender, loving disposition of the child impressed all who came in contact with her. As she advanced in her studies, notwithstanding the distinguished treatment she received, there was no perceptible alteration in her modesty and simplicity, which first attracted the notice of her mistress in the slave market.

Phillis was released from the labors ordinarily devolving upon slaves, on account of her delicate health, extraordinary talents and amiable deportment. We obtain this account from the memoir written by one of the family years after: "Mrs. Wheatley did not require or permit her services as a domestic,

but she would sometimes allow her to polish a table or dust an
apartment, or engage in some other trifling occupation that
would break in upon her sedentary habits; but not unfre-
quently in these cases the brush and the duster were soon
dropped for the pen, that her meditated verse might not escape her." The slave girl won the love of Mrs. Wheatley and
the entire household, and well repaid her mistress. Says
the writer of the memoir, further: "Phillis ate of her bread
and was to her as a daughter, for she returned her affection with unbounded gratitude, and was so devoted to her interests as to have no will in opposition to that of her benefactress."

Her manners were always unassuming and refined. There
was nothing of haughtiness or vanity about her, and her un-
fortunate kinsmen were accorded the utmost sympathy and affection. Phillis' sensitive nature led her easily to embrace
the moral lessons and teachings of the Holy Scriptures. At an
early age she gave evidence of religious experience which
characterizes all of her compositions, and was received a member of the Church of God. In the notices of her, most authors
state that she became a member of the "Old South Church" in
Boston, of which Dr. Sewell was pastor, in the year 1770,
at the age of sixteen. There is, however, accurate authority to
the effect that this event occurred one year later, on the 18th
of August, 1771; "for then," says Dr. Shurtleff, in the *Boston
Daily Advertiser* of December 21st, 1863, "under the simple
and unpretending name of Phillis, the servant of Mr. Wheatley, with no surname whatever, she became a communicant of
the 'Old South Church' in Boston, then destitute of a settled
minister, but which had lately experienced the excellent
teachings of Rev. Dr. Joseph Sewell."

That was a time when slaves were not generally baptized
into the Church. The master class justified their institution of
slavery by the declaration that they Christianized the slaves
and saved their souls, but when the slaves took them at their
word and applied for the benefits and society of the Church,
these Christian people, whose religion taught that the greatest
of Christian attributes is charity, whose Saviour taught them
to "do unto others as they would have others do unto them, "

refused to extend the right hand of fellowship to their sable
brethren.   However, be it said, as far as credit is due, that a
generous exception was made in the case of Phillis.   She was
not insensible to these prejudices, for she makes gentle references to them in several of her poems, never with bitterness of
spirit, but with true purity of heart and Christian feeling.
There is no better indication of this than can be found in the
little poem, "On being brought from Africa to America,"
and beginning thus:

"Twas mercy brought me from my Pagan land."

In the few letters remaining addressed to a fellow-slave and
dear friend, she rejoices in the "saving change" and "high
calling" with which she was favored.   During her entire life
she remained a devout and faithful Christian.

Phillis continued to advanced in her studies.   She appears
to have been well versed in sacred writings, geography, history, astronomy, ancient mythology and Latin.   She wrote
many poems and letters which have long since perished.
There appeared the first edition of her poems in Boston, 1770,
in pamphlet form, which was well received, exciting much
interest among the literary men of the period.

It has been before mentioned that Phillis was of rather delicate constitution.   The cruel separation from her parents, the
exposure to the rough scenes of the iniquitous traffic in human
beings, the severity of the Boston climate, and, in addition to
this, her intense application to study, began to tell upon the
feeble strength of the young poetess.   Mrs. Wheatley, with
almost motherly affection, became solicitous about her and
engaged the attendance of eminent physicians.   They advised
a sea-voyage.   Phillis thus had an opportunity of visiting
England.   She accompanied Mrs. Wheatley's son, Nathaniel,
who was about to visit England at that time.   He was a merchant
and purposed in the near future to take up his residence in
London.   From the date of a poem, May 7th, 1773, entitled
"A Farewell to America," to S. W. (probably Susannah
Wheatley), may be inferred the time of her departure.

Arrived in England, she was received with the highest consideration.   Her reputation, which, as we have seen, was es-
tablished in Boston, had been borne by favorable winds to the

land of England. Says George Williams, the Negro historian :
"For the previous six weeks she had cultivated her taste for
poetry, and at this time her reputation was quite well estab-
lished. She had corresponded with persons in England in
social circles, and was not a stranger to the English. She
was heartily welcomed by leaders of the society of the
British metropolis, and treated with great consideration. Under
all the trying circumstances of high social life among the nobility and rarest literary genius of London, this redeemed
child of the desert coupled to a beautiful modesty the extraordinary powers of an incomparable conversationalist. She
carried London by storm. Thoughtful people praised her; titled
people dined her, and the press extolled the name of Phillis
Wheatley, the African poetess."

At the earnest persuasions of her friends while in England,
she allowed her poetical productions to be published, and in
1773 there appeared a small octavo volume of her works, com-
prising thirty-nine poems. The book was dedicated to the
celebrated Countess of Huntingdon, and contained, besides
the poems, a picture of Phillis, a letter of introduction by her
master, John Wheatley, and a letter of recommendation by the
leading citizens of Boston. We give here a copy of these letters, as they may prove as interesting to us as they were indis-
pensable to the recognition of the African poetess. The following letter was sent by the author's master to the publisher:

"Phillis was brought from Africa to America in the year
1761, between seven and eight years of age. Without any
assistance from school education, and by only what she was
taught in .the family, she, in sixteen months time from her
arrival, attained the English language, to which she was an
utter stranger before, to such a degree as to read any of the
most difficult parts of the sacred writings, to the great astonishment of all who heard her.

"As to her writing, her own curiosty led her to it, and this
she learned in so short a time that in the year 1765 she wrote
a letter to the Rev. Mr. Occum, the Indian minister, while in
England.

"She has a great inclination to learn the Latin tongue, and

has made some progress in it.   This relation is given by her master who bought her, and with whom she now lives.

JOHN WHEATLEY."

Boston, November 14, 1772.

This was a letter written by a master of his slave, who, in genius, intellect and adaptability, was a thousand times his superior.   As this alone might not have proved sufficient to allay all doubts as to the authorship of the poems, there was a second letter published in this volume which was signed by the Governor, Lieutenant-Governor and other leading citizens of Massachusetts.   The following is a copy:

"TO THE PUBLICK."

"As it has been repeatedly suggested to the Publisher, by Persons, who have seen the Manuscript, that Numbers would be ready to suspect they were not really the writings of Phillis, he has procured the following Attestation, from the most respectable Characters in Boston, that none might have the least Ground for disputing their Origin.

We, whose names are underwritten, do assure the World, that the Poems specified in the following Pages, were (as we verily believe) written by Phillis, a young Negro Girl, who was, but a few Years since, brought, an uncultivated Barbarian, from Africa, and has ever since been, and now is, under the Disadvantage of serving as a slave in a Family in this Town. She has been examined by some of the best Judges, and is thought qualified to write them."

His Excellency, Thomas Hutchinson, Governor.
The Hon. Andrew Oliver, Lieut.-Governor.

The Hon. Thomas Hubbard,	Mr. John Wheatley, her master.
The Hon. John Irving,	The Rev. Charles Chauncy, D. D.,
The Hon. James Pitts,	The Rev. Mather Byles, D. D.,
The Hon. Harrison Gray,	The Rev. Ed. Pemberton, D. D.,
The Hon. James Bowdoin,	The Rev. Andrew Elliot, D. D.,
John Hancock, Esq.,	The Rev. Samuel Cooper, D. D.,
Joseph Green, Esq.,	The Rev. Mr. Samuel Mather,
Richard Carey, Esq.,	The Rev. Mr. John Morehead,

Phillis was royally treated in London by the Countess of Huntingdon, the Earl of Dartmouth and others equally illustrious, and would have been presented to the young monarch,

George III, had she remained in London until the court returned to St. James. In the meantime, however, letters were received from America, informing her of the declining health of her mistress who entreated her to return. Phillis lost no time in complying with the wishes of her mistress, and immediately embarked for her Boston home, bearing with her the happiest recollections of England, and many memorials from admiring friends. Among the attentions received in that fair land was a gift from the Lord Mayor of a copy of "Paradise Lost," which was sold after her death, and is now to be found in the library at Harvard.

Her health was somewhat improved by the trip though her stay had been brief. There is a letter, remaining, dated October 30th, 1773, to her friend, Obour Tanner, from which we gather this. We learn further that since her arrival she had been troubled with the asthma, and was then feeling indisposed.

Mrs. Wheatley, whose illness occurred during Phillis' visit to England, continued to decline even upon her ward's return. She had written for Phillis to come to her, and grieved much for her presence during the short period of her absence. A picture of Phillis had been sent that good woman from London, and it was always pointed out to Mrs. Wheatley's friends. It is related that on one occasion she exclaimed with motherly affection, pointing to the picture, "See! Look at my Phillis! Does she not seem as though she would speak to me?"

The presence of Phillis afforded relief and composed the longing heart of her mistress, but the Angel of Death was hovering near. Sadness and grief were in store for the household, and a future of gloom lay before the feet of Phillis. Mrs. Wheatley's illness became more serious as the days rolled by, and soon reached its culmination. The sad event of her death occurred on March 3d, 1774, when at the age of sixty-five she was summoned "to reward."

The heart of Phillis was prostrated under the blow. She bewails her loss in a very touching and pathetic letter to her friend, the noblest tribute to be had to the kind heart of her benefactress. Says this letter: "I have lately met with a great trial in the death of my mistress; let us imagine the loss of a parent, sister or brother, the tenderness of all these was united in her. I was a poor little outcast and stranger when she took me in; not only into the house, but I presently became a sharer in her most tender affections. " Happy for us that Phillis fell into the hands of such a mistress! The generous treatment and encouragement bestowed by that kind-hearted woman were equally as rare as the rising of this genius, whom kind Providence saw fit to preserve.

Mrs. Wheatley's daughter, Mary, had been married a few years before to the Rev. John Lathroy, and Phillis was virtually without a friend. She continued, however, to reside in the household, pursuing her studies and indulging the muses, but not without feeling the want of motherly sympathy and care never again to be hers.

She wrote many poems and addressed many letters to her friends. On the 26th of October, 1775, she addressed some lines and a letter to General Washington.

The letter and poem were published in *Pennsylvania Magazine* or *American Monthly Museum* for April, 1776. Sparks, the biographer of Washington, failed to find it among Washington's papers. It appears now for the first time in any collection of Phillis Wheatley's poems, for other historians following Sparks have fallen into the same error. Mr. Sparks says of it: "I have not been able to find among Washington's papers the letter and poem addressed to him. They have doubtless been lost. From the circumstance of her invoking the muse in his praise, and from the tenor of some of her printed pieces, particularly one addressed to King George seven years before, in which she compliments him on the repeal of the stamp act, it may be inferred that she was a Whig in politics after the American way of thinking; and it might be curious to see in what manner she would eulogize liberty and the rights of man, while herself, nominally at least, in bondage. " General Washington, who appears to have been much pleased with the letter and poem, before making reply to Phillis, made the following references to them in a letter to Joseph Reed, bearing date of Feburary 10th, 1776:

"I recollect nothing else worth giving you the trouble of, unless you can be amused by reading a letter and poem ad-

dressed to me by Miss Phillis Wheatley. In searching over a
parcel of papers the other day, in order to destroy such as were
useless, I brought it to light again. At first, with a view of
doing justice to her poetical genius, I had a great mind to
publish the poem; but not knowing whether it might not be
considered rather as a mark of my own vanity than as a compliment to her, I laid it aside, till I came across it again in the
manner just mentioned. ''

Somehow or other the poem did not find its way into the
public prints, and by this means alone has it been preserved.

The great soldier, in his reply to Phillis, invited the poetess
to headquarters. It is related that she actually visited the
Revolutionary camp a few days before the British evacuated
Boston, and was received with marked attention by Washington and his officers.

Another very meritorious production came from her pen
December 30th, 1776, which is not to be found in any of the
printed editions of her works. It is a poem, entitled, "On the
Capture of General Charles Lee by the British," and is repro-
duced here for the first time.

Other poems, equally demonstrative of her poetical ability,
many of which are unfortunately lost, were written and addressed to other illustrious persons. Many of her poems were
written upon request, and this probably accounts for quite a
number being funeral poems. Though particular subjects were
often assigned, yet her compositions never failed to satisfy the
most exacting and critical. In translations of Ovid or Horace,
she was happily distinguished, and in acrostics and other mat-
ters requiring literary skill she was singularly proficient. Her
habits of composition were peculiar. She would retire at
night (her room being furnished, by the kind indulgence of
her mistress, with fire, light and writing material) and often
awaken with a train of poetic fancy and ideal images which
was immediately preserved. In this way many of her efforts
were produced, thus being original, spontaneous and highly
imaginative.

This account is given of her habits by one who had every
opportunity of knowing :

" She was allowed and even encouraged to follow the leading
of her own genius; but nothing was forced upon her, noth-

ing suggested or placed before her as a lure ; her literary efforts were altogether the natural workings of her own mind. * * She did not seem to have the power of retaining the creations of her own fancy for a long time in her mind. If during the vigil of a wakeful night she amused herself by weaving a tale, she knew nothing of it in the morning ; it had vanished in the land of dreams. ''

While Phillis was continuing to astonish the literary world, and living with a degree of comfort, other sorrows were approaching. On the 12th of March, 1778, at the ripe age of seventy-two, Mr. Wheatley was called to join his beloved wife, and Phillis was thereby deprived of a kind protector. It is most probable that she gained her freedom at this time, at the death of her master, though the opinion prevails with many writers that she was emancipated in her twentieth year, the year of her mistress's decease.

Dr. Shurtleff supposes that Mrs. Lathrop, who became her owner at the decease of her father, gave Phillis her freedom ; and Sparks writes of Phillis as being '' nominally, at least, in bondage, '' at the time she addressed the lines to General Washington, which was long after the death of Mrs. Wheatley.

However, at the time of her marriage, which occurred in April, 1778, a month after the death of Mr. Wheatley, she was styled '' a free Negro. ''

Griswold states that upon the breaking up of the Wheatley family the affairs of the Revolution so engrossed the attention of acquaintances and friends that Phillis was left dependent upon herself alone ; and further, that she took an apartment and attempted in some way to support herself, but, being unsuccessful, she saw with fears the approach of poverty, and, in despair of her situation, married.

This is hardly probable, for Mrs. Lathrop was living at the time of her marriage ; nor is it likely that Phillis was influenced by aught save her affections. The name of the individual to whom she was united was John Peters. We find Phillis in one of her letters bearing the date before the death of her mistress, referring to Peters as being a very clever young man, very complacent and agreeable, and well acquainted with her friend and correspondent.

Many conflicting accounts are given of this John Peters, who according to different reports, was a grocer, barber, baker, lawyer or doctor. On the one hand, some are of the opinion that Peters was in superiority of other Negroes, a phenomenon, that he "became a lawyer under the name of Dr. Peters and placed before the tribunal the cause of the blacks;" and further, that "the reputation he enjoyed procured him a fortune. "

Another account is thus given : "She soon after received an offer of marriage from a respectable colored man of Boston. The name of this individual was John Peters. He kept a grocery in Court Street and was a man of handsome person. He wore a wig, carried a cane, and quite acted out 'the gentleman. ' In an evil hour he was accepted ; and though he was a man of talents and information, writing with fluency and propriety, and, at one period, reading law, he proved utterly unworthy of the distinguished woman who honored him by her alliance. "

On the other hand, it has been said that he was unsuccessful in business, and did not make a fortune, and that " he was too proud and indolent to apply himself to any occupation below his fancied dignity. "

All writers are agreed as to the ability and intellectual attainments of Mr. Peters. He was frequently seen in the court room of Boston, even after the demise of Phillis, though another report says he went South, carrying her papers with him, and there probably ended his days. Phillis' married life was brief, if it was not happy. In a letter to her friend, bearing date of May 10th, 1779, she writes that her health is good. We also gather from another of her letters that they resided in Queen Street, Boston, for a while at least. That Phillis continued her intellectual pursuits after marriage we have every reason to believe. Her husband, from all accounts, was most likely to encourage it. There was a proposal made (from the *Evening Post and General Advertiser* of October 30, 1779) for printing by subscription a volume of poems and letters on various subjects, dedicated to the Right Hon. Benjamin Franklin, Esq., one of the Ambassadors of the United States at the Court of France, by Phillis Peters.

Among the poems to be published in this volume were the following: "To His Excellency, General Washington," "On the Death of General Wooster," and "On the Capture of General Lee." There were thirteen letters, including correspondence to the Right Hon. William E. Dartmouth, Right Hon. Countess of Huntingdon, Dr. B. Rush of Philadelphia, Rev. Dr. Thomas of London, and others. The following notice appeared at the same time :

" The learned and ingenious, as well as those who are pleased with novelty, are invited to encourage the publication, by a generous subscription—the former that they may fan the sacred fire which is self-enkindled in the breast of this *young* African ; the ingenious, that they may, by reading this collection, have a large play for their imaginations, and be excited to please and benefit mankind by some brilliant production of their own pens—those who are always in search of some new thing that they may obtain a sight of this *rara avis in terra*—and everyone that the ingenious author may be encouraged to improve her own mind, benefit and please mankind. "

This volume was never printed, much to our regret, as many of the compositions are lost.   None of the letters for the above-proposed volume remain or have been brought to light.

The few letters in the present work were addressed to Obour Tanner, a friend and slave, probably one of the young girls brought from Africa at the same time as Phillis. She resided in Newport, and, from the high tenor of Phillis' letters, must have possessed more than ordinary intelligence.

How long Phillis remained in comfort and ease during her married life is not known. The weight of authority leads to the opinion that her husband became reduced in circumstances a few years before the death of Phillis. It is certain they removed from Boston, taking up their abode in Wilmington, in the interior of Massachusetts, until the close of the war, when they returned again to Boston. In the meantime the tender and devoted wife became an affectionate mother.   Three children were the product of this marriage, all of whom died early. Many writers err in this and in the date of her demise, stating that the poet-wife became the mother of one child, while they terminate her career in 1780, at the age of twenty-six. The best authority is here followed.

Mrs. Lathrop had died shortly after the marriage of Phillis, on the 24th of December, 1778, at the age of thirty-five, while her brother Nathaniel, who resided in England, expired in 1783. It was about the time of this latter event that Phillis lost two of her children. Her husband appears to have been unsuccessful in business, and often his family was in extreme distress and want. His pride and talents may have caused him to disdain the pursuits and methods of living common to those of inferior attainments, so that Phillis, herself tenderly reared, and of feeble constitution, was too often made a sufferer by reason of his fancied dignity. It was related that in 1784 her husband " was forced to relieve himself of debt by imprisonment in the county jail," and Phillis, in this distress, was under the neccessity of earning her own subsistence by ordinary household labors. It must be remembered that this was a period of general distress and poverty in this country. The war for independence had ruined the business interests and distroyed the fortunes of many, and most likely the impoverished condition of this family is mainly traceable to the " general hard times. "

The fragile health of the poetess did not long endure the cares and woes of wedded life. She became ill and soon succumbed to the trials, misfortunes and miseries about her, yet at no time was any word of reproach or even of complaint heard to escape her lips in evidence of unkind treatment by her husband or dissatisfaction with her lot. "And now, " says a distinguished writer, " her disease rapidly increased, and on the 5th of December, 1784, at the early age of thirty-one years, poor Phillis Peters, alias Wheatley, drew her last breath, and soon, together with her last offspring, which seems to have been left until then to make the occasion more mournful, was carried to her last earthly resting place, without one of the friends of her prosperity to follow her, and without a stone to mark her grave. "

The following notice, from the *Independent Chronicle* of the Thursday succeedifig her death, contains all that is known of the death and burial of Phillis : "Last Lord's day, died Mrs.

Phillis Peters (formerly Phillis Wheatley), aged 31, known to the literary world by her celebrated Miscellaneous Poems. Her funeral is to be this afternoon at four o'clock, from the house lately improved by Mr. Todd, nearly opposite Dr. Bullfinch's, at West Boston, where her friends and acquaintances are desired to attend."

She was greatly beloved and sincerely mourned by all who knew her. Superior by nature, impressing by her presence, charming by her conversation, exciting admiration by her talents, winning love by her tenderness, conquering prejudice by her Christianity, she commanded the hearts of the high and low, of the master and slave, and furnished the world another example of true greatness that would adorn the most cultured age.

At the early age of thirty-one years, when the rose had scarcely reached the fullness of its bloom, the reaper came that knows no sweetness, charm or love. A devout Christian in this life, her departure was equally glorious; in her own language relative to her departed mistress: "With inexpressible raptures, earnest longings and impatient thirstings for the upper courts of the Lord."

We cannot forbear mentioning a pleasing incident from Sparks' "Washington," which showed not only the appreciation of the "Father of his Country" for the poetess, but also the high estimation in which she was held in this country at that time. Phillis addressed a letter and poem to General Washington, of which further mention will be made, calling forth the following letter in reply:

"CAMBRIDGE, February 28th, 1776.

MISS PHILLIS:—Your favor of the 26th of October did not reach my hands till the middle of December. Time enough, you will say, to have given an answer ere this. Granted. But a variety of important occurrences continually interposing to distract the mind and withdraw the attention, I hope, will apologize for the delay and plead my excuse for the seeming but not real neglect. I thank you most sincerely for your polite notice of me in the elegant lines you enclosed, and however undeserving I may be of such encomium and panegyric, the style and manner exhibit a striking proof of your poetical talents; in honor of which, and as a tribute justly due to you, I would have published the poem had I not been apprehensive that, while I only meant to give the world this new instance of your genius, I might have incurred the imputation of vanity. This, and nothing else, determined me not to give it place in the public prints. If you should ever come to Cambridge, or near headquarters, I shall be happy to see a person so favored by the muses, and to whom Nature has been so liberal and beneficent in her dispensations.

I am, with great respect,

Your obedient humble servant,

" GEORGE WASHINGTON. "

This was Washington's opinion of the young poetess, the same that he had, before this, expressed in a private letter to Joseph Reed. It is a handsome compliment to Phillis, and at the same time an index of the generous nature and sympathetic heart of the old soldier.

The influence of Phillis Wheatley's writings has been quite extensive. Her poems were received with popular applause in the great cities of America and Europe. They owe their merit not to the fact that an African slave had produced them, but to the superior skill of composition, the delicacy of sentiment, the felicity of expression, and the delightful flow that bespeak no ordinary talents. That the true poet is born, her life and training bear strong testimony. Neither the education nor the religion she received on American soil raised her to the atmosphere of song. In her savage home, on "Africa's burning sands," she would have sung the triumphs of a victorious chief, or mourned the sorrows of an afflicted people. With the English language on her tongue she wrote verse the most learned Englishmen deemed worthy of praise. In the day when American poets were less numerous and illustrious, the worthiest of them was forced to divide his glory with an African slave. In the days when women were not encouraged to pursue the richer fields of science and literature, when only the wealthy and refined invaded the storehouses of ancient classics, a Negro girl became an honored precedent for an ungrateful nation.

PHILLIS WHEATLEY'S CORRESPONDENCE.

I.—To Obour Tanner,* in Newport.

BOSTON, May 19, 1772.

DEAR SISTER.—I rec'd your favour of February 6th, for which I give you my sincere thanks. I greatly rejoice with you in that realizing view, and I hope experieuce, of the saving change which you so emphatically describe. Happy were it for us if we could arrive to that evangelical repentance, and the true holiness of heart which you mention. Inexpressibly happy should we be, could we have a due sense of the beauties and excellence of the crucified Savior. In his crucifixion may be seen marvellous displays of Grace and Love, sufficient to draw and invite us to the rich and endless treasures of his mercy; let us rejoice in and adore the wonders of God's infinite Love in bringing us from a land semblant of darkness itself, and where the divine light of revelation (being obscured) is in darkness. Here the knowledge of the true God and eternal life are made manifest; but there profound ignorance overshadows the land. Your observation is true, namely, that there was nothing in us to recommend us to God. Many of our fellow-creatures were pass'd by, when the bowels of divine love expanded towards us. May this goodness & long suffering of God lead us to unfeign'd repentance.

It gives me great pleasure to hear of so many of my nation seeking with eagerness the way to true felicity. O may we all meet at length in that happy mansion. I hope the correspondence between us will continue (my being much indispos'd this Winter past was the reason of my not answering yours before now), which correspondence I hope may have the happy effect of improving our mutual friendship. Till we meet in the region of consummate blessedness, let us endeavor, by the assistance of divine grace, to live the life, and we shall die the death of the Righteous. May this be our happy case, and of those who are travelling to the region of Felicity, is the earnest request of your affectionate

Friend & Humble servant

PHILLIS WHEATLEY.

---

*Obour Tanner, the person to whom these letters were addressed, was a fellow-slave, a friend of Phillis', probably an African, and one of the girls brought over at the same time with Phillis. She lived till 1833 or '34, and was described as "an uncommonly pious, sensible and intelligent woman, respected and visited by every person in Newport who could appreciate excellence."

2.—To Obour Tanner, in Newport, Rhode Island.
To the Care of Mr. Pease's Servant.

Boston, July 19th, 1772.

My Dear Friend.—I rec'd your kind epistle a few days ago; much disappointed to hear that you had not received my answer to your first letter. I have been in a very poor state of health all the past winter and spring, and now reside in the country for the benefit of its more wholesome air. I came to town this morning to spend the Sabbath with my master and mistress. Let me be interested in your prayers that God would please to bless to me the means us'd for my recovery, if agreeable to his holy will. While my outward man languishes under weakness and pa[in], may the inward be refresh'd and strengthen'd more abundantly by him who declar'd from heaven that his strength was made perfect in weakness! May he correct our vitiated taste, that the meditation of him may be delightful to us, no longer to be so excessively charm'd with fleeting vanities; but pressing forward to the fix'd mark for the prize. How happy that man who is prepar'd for that night wherein no man can work! Let us be mindful of our high calling, continually on our guard, lest our treacherous hearts should give the adversary an advantage over us. O! who can think without horror of the snares of the Devil. Let us by frequent meditation on the eternal Judgment prepare for it. May the Lord bless to us these thoughts, and teach us by his Spirit to live to him alone, and when we leave this world may we be his. That this may be our happy case, is the sincere desire of

Your affectionate friend & humble serv't,

PHILLIS WHEATLEY.

3.—To Obour Tanner, in Newport.

Boston, October 30, 1773.

Dear Obour,—I rec'd your most kind epistles of Augt. 27th & Oct. 13th by a young man of your acquaintance, for which I am ablig'd to you. I hear of your welfare with pleasure; but this acquaints you that I am at present indispos'd by a cold, & since my arrival have been visited by the asthma.

Your observations on our dependence on the Diety, & your hope that my wants will be supply'd from his fulness which is in Christ Jesus, is truly worthy of yourself. I can't say but my voyage to England has conduced to the recovery (in a great measure) of my health. The friends I found there among the nobility and gentry, their benevolent conduct towards me, the unexpected and unmerited civility and complaisance with which I was treated by all, fill me with astonishment. I can scarcely realize it. This I humbly hope has the happy effect of lessening me in my own esteem. Your reflections on the sufferings of the Son of God, & the inestimable price of our immortal souls, plainly demonstrate the sensations of a soul united to Jesus. What you observe of Esau is true of all mankind, who (left to themselves) would sell their heavenly birth rights for a few moments of sensual pleasure, whose wages at last (dreadful wages!) is eternal condemnation. Dear Obour, let us not sell our birth right for a thousand worlds, which indeed would be as dust upon the balance. The God of the seas and dry land, has graciously brought me home in safety. Join with me in thanks to him for so great a mercy, & that it may excite me to praise him with cheerfulness, to persevere in Grace & Faith, & in the knowledge of our Creator & Redeemer—that my heart may be fill'd with gratitude. I should have been pleas'd greatly to see Miss West, as I imagine she knew you. I have been very busy ever since my arrival, or should have now written a more particular account of my voyage, but must submit that satisfaction to some other opportunity.

          I am Dear friend

               Most affectionately ever yours

                         PHILLIS WHEATLEY.

My mistress has been very sick above 14 weeks, & confined to her bed the whole time, but is I hope somewhat better now

The young man* by whom this is handed you seems to me to be a very clever man, knows you very well, & is very complaisant and agreeable.   P. W.

I enclose Proposals for my book and beg you'd use your interest to get subscriptions, as it is for my benefit.

4.—TO MISS OBOUR TANNER, NEWPORT, RHODE ISLAND.

               BOSTON, March 21, 1774.

DEAR OBOUR—I rec'd your obliging letter, enclos'd in your rev'd. Pastor's and handed me by his son. I have lately met with a great trial in the death of my mistress; let us imagine the loss of a parent, sister, or brother, the tenderness of all these were united in her. I was a poor little outcast and a stranger when she took me in; not only into her house, but I presently became a sharer in her most tender affections. I was treated

---

*The young man referred to is John Peters, who afterward became her husband.

by her more like her child than her servant; no opportunity was left unimproved of giving me the best of advice; but in terms how tender! how engaging! This I hope ever to keep in remembrance. Her exemplary life was a greater monitor than all her precepts and instruction; thus we may observe of how much greater force example is than instruction. To alleviate our sorrows we had the satisfaction to see her depart in inexpressible raptures, earnest longings, and impatient thirstings for the upper courts of the Lord. Do, my dear friend, remember me and this family in your closet, that this afflicting dispensation may be sanctify'd to us.

I am very sorry to hear that you are indispos'd, but hope this will find you in better health. I have been unwell the greater part of the winter, but am much better as the spring approaches. Pray excuse my not writing to you so long before, for I have been so busy lately that I could not find leisure. I shall send the 5 books you wrote for, the first convenient opportunity; if you want more, they shall be ready for you. I am very affectionately

Your friend

PHILLIS WHEATLEY.

5.—To MISS OBOUR TANNER, NEWPORT, RHODE ISLAND,
fav'd by Mr. Pemberton.

DEAR OBOUR.—I rec'd last evening your kind & friendly letter and am not a little animated thereby. I hope ever to follow your good advices and be resigned to the afflicting hand of a seemingly frowning Providence. I have rec'd the money you sent for the 5 books, & 2-6 more for another, which I now send & wish safe to hand. Your tenderness for my welfare demands my gratitude. Assist me, dear Obour! to praise our great benefactor, for the innumerable benefits continually pour'd upon me, that while he strikes one comfort *dead* he raises up another. But O that I could dwell on & delight in him alone above every other object! while the world hangs loose about us we shall not be in painful *anxiety* in giving up to God that which he first gave to us. Your letter came by Mr. Pemberton who brings you the book you wrote for. I shall wait on Mr. Whitwell with your letter, and am

Dear Sister, ever affectionately, your

PHILLIS WHEATLEY.

I have rec'd by some, of the last ship, 300 more of my Poems.

BOSTON, May 6, 1774.

6.—MISS OBOUR TANNER, WORCESTER.

BOSTON, May 29th-'78.

DEAR OBOUR.—I am exceedingly glad to hear from you by Mrs. Tanner, and wish you had timely notice of her departure, so as to have written me; next to that is the pleasure of hearing that you are well. The vast variety of scenes that have pass'd before us these 3 years past, will to a reasonable mind serve to convince us of the uncertain duration of all things temporal, and the proper result of such a consideration is an ardent desire of, & preparation for, a state and enjoyments which are more suitable to the immortal mind.

You will do me a great favour if you'll write me by every opportunity. Direct your letters under cover to Mr. John Peters, in Queen Street. I have but half an hour's notice; and must apologize for this hasty scrawl.

I am most affectionately, my dear Obour, your sincere friend   PHILLIS WHEATLEY.

7.—MISS OBOUR TANNER, WORCESTER,
fav'd by Cumberland.

BOSTON, May 10, 1779.

DR. OBOUR —By this opportunity I have the pleasure to inform you that I am well and hope you are so; tho' I have been silent, I have not been unmindful of you, but a variety of hindrances was the cause of my not writing to you. But in time to come, I hope our correspondence will revive————and revive in better times————pray write me soon, for I long to hear from you————You may depend on constant replies ————I wish you much happiness, and am

Dr. Obour, your friend & sister

PHILLIS PETERS.

---

*   8.—TO HIS EXCELLENCY, GENERAL WASHINGTON.

SIR,

I have taken the freedom to address your Excellency in the enclosed poem, and entreat your acceptance, though I am not insensible of its inaccuracies.

Your being appointed by the Grand Continental Congress to be Generalissimo of the armies of North America, together with the fame of your virtues, excites sensations not easy to suppress. Your generosity, therefore, I presume, will pardon the attempt. Wishing your Excellency all possible success in the great cause you are so generously engaged in, I am

Your Excellency's most obedient humble servant,

PHILLIS WHEATLEY.

PROVIDENCE, Oct. 26, 1775.

To His Excellency, Gen. Washington.

Celestial choir! enthron'd in realms of light,
Columbia's scenes of glorious toils I write.
While freedom's cause her anxious breast alarms,
She flashes dreadful in refulgent arms.
See mother Earth her offspring's fate bemoan
And nations gaze at scenes before unknown!
See the bright beams of heaven's revolving light
Involved in sorrows and the veil of night!
The goddess comes, she moves divinely fair,
Olive and laurel bind her golden hair;
Wherever shines this native of the skies,
Unnumber'd charms and recent graces rise.
Muse! how propitious while my pen relates
How pour her armies through a thousand gates,
As when Eolus heaven's fair face deforms,
Enwrapp'd in tempest and a night of storms;
Astonish'd ocean feels the wild uproar
The refluent surges beat the sounding shore;
Or thick as leaves in Autumn's golden reign
Such and so many moves the warriors' train.
In bright array they seek the work of war
Where high unfurl'd the ensign waves in air.
Shall I to Washington their praise recite?
Enough thou knowest them in the field of fight.
Thee first in place and honours—we demand
The grace and glory of thy martial band.
Fam'd for thy valour, for thy virtues more,
Hear every tongue thy guardian aid implore!
One century scarce perform'd its destin'd round
When Gallic powers Columbia's fury found;
And so may you whoever dares disgrace
The land of freedom's heaven-defended race!
Fix'd are the eyes of nations on the scales
For in their hopes Columbia's arm prevails,
Anon Britannia droops the pensive head,
While round increase the rising hills of dead.
Ah! cruel blindness to Columbia's state!
Lament thy thrift of boundless power too late.
Proceed, great chief, with virtue on thy side
Thy ev'ry action let the goddess guide.
A crown, a mansion and a throne that shine
With gold unfading, Washington, be thine.

---

* This letter and poem called forth a reply from Gen. Washington
highly complimentary to the talented author.

Poem on the Capture of Gen. Charles Lee
by the British.

"The following thoughts on his Excellency Major General Lee being betray'd into the hands of the Enemy by the treachery of a pretended Friend; To the Honorable James Bowdoin, Esqr., are most respectfully Inscrib'd,

By his most obedient and devoted humble servant,

PHILLIS WHEATLEY."

" The deed perfidious and the Hero's fate
In tender strains, celestial Muse! relate.
The latent foe to friendship makes pretense,
The name assumed without the sacred sense!
He, with a rapture well dissembl'd, pressed
The hero's hand, and, fraudful, thus address'd,
'O friend belov'd! May heaven its aid afford,
And spread yon troops beneath thy conquering sword!
Grant to America's united prayer
A glorious conquest on the field of war!
But thou indulgent to my warm request,
Vouchsafe thy presence as my honour'd guest:
From martial cares a space unbend thy soul
In social banquet, and the sprightly bowl. '
Thus spoke the foe: and war-like Lee reply'd,
'Ill fits it me, who such an army guide,
To whom his conduct each brave soldier owes,
To waste an hour in banquets or repose;
This day important, with loud voice demands,
Our wisest counsels, and our bravest hands. '
Thus having said, he heav'd a boding sigh;
The hour approach'd that damps Columbia's joy.
Inform'd, conducted by the treach'rous friend.
With winged speed the adverse train attend,
Ascend the Dome, and seize with frantic air
The self-surrender'd glorious prize of war!
On sixty coursers, swifter than the wind
They fly and reach the British camp assign'd.
Arriv'd, what transport touched their leader's breast!
Who, thus deriding, the brave Chief address'd:
'Say art thou he, beneath whose vengeful hands
Our best of heroes grasp'd in death the sand?
One fierce regard of thine indignant eye
Turn'd Britain pale, and made her armies fly:
But oh! how changed! a prisoner in our arms
Till martial honour, dreadful in her charms,
Shall grace Britannia at her son's return

And widow'd thousands in our triumphs mourn.'
While thus he spoke the hero of renown
Survey'd the boaster with a gloomy frown
And stern reply'd, 'O arrogance of tongue !
And wild ambition ever prone to wrong !
Believ'st thou, chief, that armies such as thine
Can stretch in dust that heaven-defended line ?
In vain allies may swarm from distant lands,
And demons aid in formidable bands.
Great as thou art, thou shun'st the field of fame
Disgrace to Britain and to the British name !
When offer'd combat by the noble foe,
(Foe to mis-rule) why did thy sword forego
The easy conquest of the rebel land ?
Perhaps too easy for thy martial hand,
What various causes to the field invite !
For plunder you, and we for freedom fight.
Her cause divine with generous ardour fires
And every bosom glows as she inspires !
Already thousands of your troops are fled
To the dread mansions of the silent dead;
Columbia, too, beholds with streaming eyes
Her heroes fall—'tis Freedom's sacrifice !
So wills the Power who with convulsive storms
Shakes impious realms and nature's face deforms;
Yet those brave troops, innum'rous as the sands,
One soul inspires, one General Chief commands
Find in your train of boasted heroes one
To match the praise of Godlike Washington.
Thrice happy Chief ! in whom the virtues join,
And heaven-taught prudence speaks the man divine !'
He ceased. Amazement struck the warrior train
And doubt of conquest on the hostile plain. "

BOSTON. Dec. 30, 1776.

PHILLIS WHEATLEY'S POEMS

[Title Page of the First Edition of Phillis Wheatley's Poems]

POEMS

O N

VARIOUS SUBJECTS

RELIGIOUS AND MORAL

B Y

PHILLIS WHEATLEY

NEGRO SERVANT to MR. JOHN WHEATLEY,

of BOSTON, in NEW ENGLAND.

LONDON:

Printed for A. BELL, Bookseller, Aldgate ; and sold by
Messrs. COX and BERRY, King-Street, BOSTON.

MDCCLXXIII.

[Dedication of the First Edition of Phillis Wheatley's Poems]

DEDICATION.

To the Right Honourable the

COUNTESS OF HUNTINGDON,

THE FOLLOWING

POEMS

Are most respectfully

Inscribed,

By her much obliged,

Very humble,

And devoted Servant,

Phillis Wheatley.

Boston, June 12,
1773.

PREFACE.

THE following Poems were written originally for the Amusement of the Author, as they were the Products of her leisure Moments. She had no Intention ever to have published them; nor would they now have made their Appearance, but at the Importunity of many of her best, and most generous Friends ; to whom she considers herself, as under the greatest Obligations.

As her Attempts in Poetry are now sent into the World, it is hoped the Critic will not severely censure their Defects ; and we presume they have too much Merit to be cast aside with Contempt, as worthless and trifling Effusions.

As to the Disadvantages she has laboured under, with Regard to Learning, nothing needs to be offered, as her Master's Letter will sufficiently shew the Difficulties in this Respect she had to encounter.

With all their Imperfections, the Poems are now humbly submitted to the Perusal of the Public.

PHILLIS WHEATLEY'S POEMS

POEMS

O N

VARIOUS SUBJECTS.

To Maecenas.

MÆCENAS, you, beneath the myrtle shade,
 Read o'er what poets sung, and shepherds play'd-
What felt those poets, but you feel the same?
Does not your soul possess the sacred flame?
Their noble strains your equal genius shares
In softer language and diviner airs.

 While Homer paints, lo! circumfus'd in air,
Celestial Gods in mortal forms appear;
Swift as they move hear each recess rebound,
Heav'n quakes, earth trembles, and the shores resound.
Great sire of verse, before my mortal eyes,
The lightnings blaze across the vaulted skies,
And, as the thunder shakes the heavenly plains,
A deep-felt horror thrills through all my veins.
When gentler strains demand thy graceful song,
The length'ning line moves languishing along.
When great Patroclus courts Achilles' aid,
The grateful tribute of my tears is paid;
Prone on the shore he feels the pangs of love,
And stern Pelides' tend'rest passions move.

Great Maro's strain in heavenly numbers flows,
The Nine inspire, and all the bosom glows.
O could I rival thine and Virgil's page,
Or claim the Muses with the Mantuan Sage ;
Soon the same beauties should my mind adorn,
And the same ardors in my soul should burn :
Then should my song in bolder notes arise,
And all my numbers pleasingly surprise ;
But here I sit, and mourn a grov'ling mind,
That fain would mount, and ride upon the wind.

Not you, my friend, these plaintive strains become,
Not you, whose bosom is the Muses' home ;
When they from tow'ring Helicon retire,
They fan in you the bright immortal fire,
But I, less happy, cannot raise the song,
The falt'ring music dies upon my tongue.

The happier Terrence* all the choir inspir'd,
His soul replenish'd and his bosom fir'd ;
But say, ye Muses, why this partial grace,
To one alone of Afric's sable race ;
From age to age transmitting thus his name
With the first glory in the rolls of fame ?

Thy virtues, great Mæcenas ! shall be sung
In praise of him, from whom those virtues sprung ;
While blooming wreaths around thy temples spread,
I'll snatch a laurel from thine honour'd head,
While you indulgent smile upon the deed.

*He was an African by birth.

As long as Thames in streams majestic flows,
Or Naiads in their oozy beds repose,
While Phœbus reigns above the starry train,
While bright Aurora purples o'er the main,
So long, great Sir, the muse thy praise shall sing,
So long thy praise shall make Parnassus ring;
Then grant, Mæcenas, thy paternal rays,
Hear me propitious, and defend my lays.

On Virtue.

O THOU bright jewel, in my aim I strive
To comprehend thee. Thine own words declare
Wisdom is higher than a fool can reach.
I cease to wonder, and no more attempt
Thine height t' explore, or fathom thy profound.
But, O my soul, sink not into despair,
Virtue is near thee, and with gentle hand
Would now embrace thee, hovers o'er thine head.
Fain would the heaven-born soul with her converse,
Then seek, then court her for her promis'd bliss.

Auspicious queen, thine heavenly pinions spread,
And lead celestial Chastity along;
Lo! now her sacred retinue descends,
Array'd in glory from the orbs above.
Attend me, Virtue, through my youthful years!
O leave me not to the false joys of time!
But guide my steps to endless life and bliss.

Greatness, or Goodness, say what I shall call thee,
To give an higher appellation still,
Teach me a better strain, a nobler lay,
O thou, enthroned with cherubs in the realms of day !

To the University of Cambridge, in New England.

WHILE an intrinsic ardor prompts to write,
    The muses promise to assist my pen ;
        'Twas not long since I left my native shore,
The land of errors, and Egyptian gloom :
Father of mercy, 'twas thy gracious hand
Brought me in safety from those dark abodes.

    Students, to you 'tis given to scan the heights
Above, to traverse the ethereal space,
And mark the systems of revolving worlds.
Still more, ye sons of science, ye receive
The blissful news of messengers from heav'n,
How Jesus' blood for your redemption flows.
See him with hands outstretcht upon the cross ;
Immense compassion in his bosom glows ;
He hears revilers, nor resents their scorn :
What matchless mercy in the Son of God !
When the whole human race by sin had fallen,
He deigned to die that they might rise again,
And share with him in the sublimest skies,
Life without death, and glory without end.

46

Improve your privileges while they stay,
Ye pupils, and each hour redeem, that bears
Or good or bad report of you to heaven.
Let sin, that baneful evil to the soul,
By you be shunned, nor once remit your guard ;
Suppress the deadly serpent in its egg.
Ye blooming plants of human race divine,
An Ethiop tells you 'tis your greatest foe ;
Its transient sweetness turns to endless pain,
And in immense perdition sinks the soul.

To the King's Most Excellent Majesty, 1768.

YOUR subjects hope, dread Sire—
    The crown upon your head may flourish long,
        And that your arm may in your God be strong !
O may your sceptre num'rous nations sway,
And all with love and readiness obey !

    But how shall we the British King reward ?
Rule thou in peace, our father, and our lord !
Midst the remembrance of thy favors past,
The meanest peasants most admire the last.*
May George, belov'd by all the nations round,
Live with heaven's choicest blessings crown'd !
Great God, direct, and guard him from on high,
And from his head let every evil fly !
And may each clime with equal gladness see
A monarch's smile can set his subjects free !

*The Repeal of the Stamp Act.

On Being Brought From Africa to America.

TWAS mercy brought me from my Pagan land,
    Taught my benighted soul to understand
        That there's a God, that there's a Saviour too.
Once I redemption neither sought nor knew.
Some view our sable race with scornful eye ;
"Their colour is a diabolic dye."
Remember, Christians, Negroes, black as Cain,
May be refined, and join the angelic train.

On the Death of Rev. Dr. Sewell, 1769.

ERE yet the morn its lovely blushes spread,
    See Sewell number'd with the happy dead.
        Hail happy man, arriv'd th' immortal shore,
Though we shall hear thy warning voice no more,
Come, let us all behold with wistful eyes
The saint ascending to his native skies ;
From hence the prophet wing'd his rapt'rous way
To the blest mansions of eternal day.
Then begging for the Spirit of our God,
And panting eager for the same abode,
Come, let us all with the same vigor rise,
And take a prospect of the blissful skies ;
While on our minds Christ's image is imprest,
And the dear Saviour glows in every breast.
Thrice happy saint ! to find thy heav'n at last,
What compensation for the evils past !

Great God, incomprehensible, unknown
By sense, we bow at thine exalted throne.
O, while we beg thine excellence to feel,
Thy sacred Spirit to our hearts reveal,
And give us of that mercy to partake,
Which Thou hast promised for the Saviour's sake !

  "Sewell is dead," swift-pinion'd Fame thus cry'd.
"Is Sewell dead?" my trembling tongue reply'd.
O, what a blessing in his flight deny'd !
How oft for us that holy prophet pray'd !
How oft to us the Word of Life convey'd !
By duty urg'd my mournful verse to close,
I for his tomb this epitaph compose :

  "Lo, here a man, redeem'd by Jesus' blood,
"A sinner once, but now a saint with God ;
"Behold, ye rich, ye poor, ye fools, ye wise,
"Nor let his monument your heart surprise ;
"'Twill tell you what this holy man has done,
"Which gives him brighter lustre than the sun.
"Listen, ye happy, from your seats above.
"I speak sincerely, while I speak and love,
"He sought the paths of piety and truth,
"By these made happy from his early youth ;
"In glooming years that grace divine he felt,
"Which rescues sinners from the chains of guilt.
"Mourn him, ye indigent, whom he has fed,
"And henceforth seek, like him, for living bread ;
"Ev'n Christ, the bread descending from above,
"And ask an int'rest in his saving love.

"Mourn him, ye youth, to whom he oft has told
"God's gracious wonders from the times of old.
"I too have cause this mighty loss to mourn,
"For he, my monitor, will not return.
"O when shall we to his blest state arrive ?
"When the same graces in our bosoms thrive."

On the Death of the Rev. Mr. George Whitefield, 1770.

HAIL, happy saint, on thine immortal throne,
Possest of glory, life and bliss unknown ;
We hear no more the music of thy tongue,
Thy wonted auditories cease to throng.
Thy sermons in unequall'd accents flow'd,
And ev'ry bosom with devotion glow'd ;
Thou didst in strains of eloquence refin'd
Inflame the heart and captivate the mind.
Unhappy we the setting sun deplore,
So glorious once, but ah ! it shines no more.
  Behold the prophet in his tow'ring flight !
He leaves the earth for heav'n's unmeasur'd height,
And worlds unknown receive him from our sight.
There Whitefield wings with rapid course his way,
And sails to Zion through vast seas of day.
Thy pray'rs, great saint, and thine incessant cries
Have pierc'd the bosom of thy native skies.
Thou, moon, hast seen and all the stars of light,
How he has wrestled with his God by night.

He pray'd that grace in ev'ry heart might dwell,
He long'd to see America excel :
He charg'd its youth that ev'ry grace divine
Should with full lustre in their conduct shine :
That Saviour, which his soul did first receive,
The greatest gift that ev'n a God can give,
He freely offer'd to the num'rous throng,
That on his lips with list'ning pleasure hung.

   "Take him, ye wretched, for your only good,
"Take him, ye starving sinners, for your food.
"Ye thrifty, come to this life-giving stream,
"Ye preachers, take him for your joyful theme ;
"Take him, my dear Americans, he said,
"Be your complaints on his kind bosom laid ;
"Take him, ye Africans, he longs for you,
"Impartial Saviour is his title due ;
"Washed in the fountain of redeeming blood,
"You shall be sons and kings, and Priests to God."

   Great Countess,* we Americans revere
Thy name, and mingle in thy grief sincere ;
New England deeply feels, the Orphans mourn,
Their more than father will no more return.
But, though arrested by the hand of death,
Whitefield no more exerts his lab'ring breath,
Yet let us view him in th' eternal skies,
Let ev'ry heart to this bright vision rise ;
While the tomb safe retains its sacred trust,
Till life divine re-animates his dust.

*The Countess of Huntingdon, to whom Mr. Whitefield was chaplain.

On the Death of a Young Lady of Five Years of Age.

FROM dark abodes to fair ethereal light
    Th' enraptured innocent has wing'd her flight;
    On the kind bosom of eternal love
She finds unknown beatitude above.
This know, ye parents, nor her loss deplore,
She feels the iron hand of pain no more;
The dispensations of unerring grace,
Should turn your sorrows into grateful praise;
Let then no tears for her henceforward flow,
No more distress in our dark vale below.
    Her morning sun, which rose divinely bright,
Was quickly mantled with the gloom of night;
But hear in heav'n's blest bow'rs your Nancy fair,
And learn to imitate her language there.
"Thou, Lord, whom I behold with glory crown'd
"By what sweet name, and in what tuneful sound
"Wilt thou be prais'd? Seraphic pow'rs are faint,
"Infinite love and majesty to paint.
"To thee let all their graceful voices raise,
"And saints and angels join their songs of praise."
    Perfect in bliss she from her heav'nly home
Looks down, and smiling beckons you to come:
Why then, fond parents, why these fruitless groans?
Restrain your tears, and cease your plaintive moans,
Freed from a world of sin, and snares, and pain,
Why would you wish your daughter back again?
No—bow resign'd. Let hope your grief control,

And check the rising tumult of the soul.
Calm in the prosperous, and adverse day,
Adore the God who gives and takes away ;
Eye him in all, His holy name revere,
Upright your actions and your hearts sincere.
'Till having sail'd through life's tempestuous sea,
And from its rocks, and boist'rous billows free,
Yourselves, safe landed on the blissful shore,
Shall join your happy babe to part no more.

On the Death of a Young Gentleman.

WHO taught thee conflict with the pow'rs of night,
To vanquish Satan in the fields of fight ?
Who strung thy feeble arms with might unknown,
How great thy conquest, and how bright thy crown !
War with each princedom, throne and pow'r is o'er,
The scene is ended to return no more.
O, could my muse thy seat on high behold,
How decked with laurel, how enrich'd with gold !
O could she hear what praise thine harp employs,
How sweet thine anthems, how divine thy joys !
What heav'nly grandeur should exalt her strain !
What holy raptures in her numbers reign !
To soothe the troubles of the mind to peace,
To still the tumult of life's tossing seas,
To ease the anguish of the parent heart,
What shall my sympathizing verse impart ?
Where is the balm to heal so deep a wound ?
Where shall a sovereign remedy be found ?

Look, gracious Spirit, from thine heav'nly bow'r,
And thy full joys into their bosoms pour;
The raging tempest of their grief control,
And spread the dawn of glory through the soul,
To eye the path the saint departed trod,
And trace him to the bosom of his God.

To a Lady on the Death of Her Husband.

GRIM monarch ! see, deprived of vital breath
  A young physician in the dust of death !
    Dost thou go on incessant to destroy ?
The grief to double and lay waste the joy ?
Enough thou never yet wast known to say
Tho' millions die the vassals of thy sway.
Nor youth, nor science, nor the ties of love,
Nor aught on earth thy flinty heart can move.
The friend, the spouse, from his dire dart to save,
In vain we ask the sovereign of the grave.
Fair mourner, there see thy lov'd Leonard laid,
And o'er him spread the deep impervious shade;
Clos'd are his eyes and heavy fetters keep
His senses bound in never-waking sleep,
Till time shall cease, till many a starry world,
Shall fall from heav'n, in dire confusion hurl'd;
Till Nature in her final wreck shall lie,
Till her last groan shall rend the azure sky:
Not till then his active soul shall claim,
His body, a divine immortal frame.

But, see the softly stealing tears apace,
Pursue each other down the mourner's face;
But cease thy tears, bid ev'ry sigh depart,
And cast the load of anguish from thine heart ;
From the cold shell of his great soul arise,
And look beyond, thou native of the skies !
There fix thy view where fleeter than the wind
Thy Leonard mounts, and leaves the earth behind.
Thyself prepare to pass the vale of night,
To join forever on the hills of light ;
To thine embrace, this joyful spirit moves,
To thee, the partner of his earthly loves ;
He welcomes thee to pleasures more refin'd
And better suited to th' immortal mind.

Goliath of Gath.

I Samnel, Chapter XVII.

YE martial pow rs, and all ye tuneful nine,
    Inspire my song, and aid my high design.
        The dreadful scenes and toils of war I write,
The ardent warriors, and the fields of fight :
You best remember, and you best can sing
The acts of heroes to the vocal string :
Resume the lays with which your sacred lyre,
Did then the poet and the sage inspire.

Now front to front the armies were display'd,
Here Israel rang'd, and there the foes array'd;
The hosts on two opposing mountains stood,
Thick as the foliage of the waving wood;
Between them an extensive valley lay,
O'er which the gleaming armor pour'd the day,
When from the camp of the Philistine foes,
Dreadful to view, a mighty warrior rose;
In the dire deeds of bleeding battle skill'd,
The monster stalks the terror of the field.
From Gath he sprung, Goliath was his name,
Of fierce deportment, and gigantic frame:
A brazen helmet on his head was plac'd,
A coat of mail his form terrific grac'd,
The greaves his legs, the targe his shoulders prest:
Dreadful in arms high-tow'ring o'er the rest
A spear he proudly wav'd, whose iron head,
Strange to relate, six hundred shekels weigh'd;
He strode along and shook the ample field,
While Phoebus blaz'd refulgent on his shield,
Through Jacob's race a chilling horror ran,
When thus the huge, enormous chief began;

　　"Say, what the cause that in this proud array
"You set your battle in the face of day?
"One hero find in all your vaunting train,
"Then see who loses, and who wins the plain;
"For he who wins, in trumph may demand
"Perpetual service from the vanquish'd land:
"Your armies I defy, your force despise,
"By far inferior in Philistia's eyes:

"Produce a man, and let us try the fight,
Decide the contest, and the victor's right."
 Thus challeng'd he; all Israel stood amaz'd,
And ev'ry chief in consternation gaz'd;
But Jesse's son in youthful bloom appears,
And warlike courage far beyond his years:
He left the folds, he left the flow'ry meads,
And soft recesses of the sylvan shades.
Now Israel's monarch, and his troops arise,
With peals of shouts ascending to the skies;
In Elah's vale the scene of combat lies,
 When the far morning flushed with Orient red,
What David's sire enjoin'd the son obey'd,
And swift of foot towards the trench he came,
Where glow'd each bosom with the martial flame.
He leaves his carriage to another's care,
And runs to greet his brethren of the war.
While yet they spake the giant-chief arose.
Repeats his challenge, and insults his foes:
Struck with the sound, and trembling at the view,
Affrighted Israel from its post withdrew.
"Observe ye this tremendous foe, they cry'd,
"Who in proud vaunts our armies hath defy'd:
"Whoever lays him prostrate on the plain,
"Freedom in Israel for his house shall gain;
"And on him wealth unknown the king will pour,
"And give his royal daughter for his dow'r."
 Then Jesse's youngest hope: "My brethren say,
"What shall be done for him who takes away
"Reproach from Jacob, who destroys the chief,

57

"And puts a period to his country's grief.
"He vaunts the honours of his arms abroad,
"And scorns the armies of the living God."
   Thus spoke the youth, th' attentive people ey'd
The wond'rous hero, again reply'd:
"Such the rewards our monarch will bestow,
"On him who conquers, and destroys his foe."
Eliab heard, and kindled into ire
   To hear his shepherd brother thus inquire,
And thus begun: "What errand brought thee? say
"Who keeps thy flock? or does it go astray?
"I know the base ambition of thine heart,
"But back in safety from the field depart."
   Eliab thus to Jesse's youngest heir,
Express'd his wrath in accents most severe.
When to his brother mildly he reply'd,
"What have I done or what the cause to chide?"
   The words were told before the king, who sent
For the young hero to his royal tent:
Before the monarch dauntless he began,
"For this Philistine fail no heart of man:
"I'll take the vale, and with the giant fight,
"I dread not all his boasts, nor all his might."
When thus the king: "Dar'st thou a stripling go,
"And venture combat with so great a foe?
"Who all his days has been inur'd to fight.
"And made its deeds his study and delight:
"Battles and bloodshed brought the monster forth,
"And clouds and whirlwinds usher'd in his birth."
When David thus: "I kept the fleecy care,
"And out there rush'd a lion and a bear;

"A tender lamb the hungry lion took,
"And with no other weapon than my crook
"Both I pursu'd, and chas'd him o'er the field,
"The prey deliver'd, and the felon kill'd:
"As thus the lion and the bear I slew,
"So shall Goliath fall, and all his crew:
"The God, who sav'd me from these beasts of prey,
"By me this monster in the dust shall lay."
So David spoke. The wond'ring king reply'd:
"Go thou with heav'n and vict'ry on thy side;
"This coat of mail, this sword gird on," he said,
And plac'd a mighty helmet on his head:
The coat, the sword, the helmet he laid aside,
Nor chose to venture with those arms untry'd,
Then took his staff, and to the neighb'ring brook
Instant he ran, and thence five pebbles took,
Meantime descended to Philistia's son
A radiant cherub, and he thus begun:
"Goliath, well thou know'st thou hast defy'd
"Yon Hebrew armies, and their God deny'd:
"Rebellious wretch! audacious worm! forbear,
"Nor tempt the vengeance of their God too far:
"Them, who with his Omnipotence contend,
"No eye shall pity, and no arm defend:
"Proud as thou art, in short-liv'd glory great,
"I come to tell thee thine approaching fate.
"Regard my words. The judge of all the gods,
"Beneath whose steps the tow'ring mountain nods,
"Will give thine armies to the savage brood,
"That cut the liquid air or range the wood.

"Thee, too, a well-aim'd pebble shall destroy,
"And thou shalt perish by a beardless boy :
"Such is the mandate from the realms above,
"And should I try the vengeance to remove
"Myself a rebel to my king would prove.
"Goliath, say, shall grace to him be shown,
"Who dares heav'ns Monarch, and insults his throne ?"

   "Your words are lost on me," the giant cries,
While fear and wrath contended in his eyes,
When thus the messenger from heav'n replies :
"Provoke no more Jehovah's awful hand
"To hurl its vengeance on thy guilty land :
"He grasps the thunder, and, he wings the storm,
"Servants their sov'reign's orders to perform."
The Angel spoke, and turn'd his eyes away,
Adding new radiance to the rising day.

   Now David comes :   The fatal stones demand
His left, the staff engag'd his better hand :
The giant mov'd, and from his tow'ring height
Survey'd the stripling, and disdain'd the fight,
And thus began : "Am I a dog with thee ?
"Bring'st thou no armour, but a staff to me ?
"The gods on thee their vollied curses pour,
"And beasts and birds of prey thy flesh devour."

   David undaunted thus, "Thy spear and shield
"Shall no protection to thy body yield :
"Jehovah's name—no other arms I bear,
"I ask no other in this glorious war.
"To-day the Lord of Hosts to me will give
"Vict'ry, to-day thy doom thou shalt receive;

"The fate you threaten shall your own become,
"And beasts shall be your animated tomb,
"That all the earth's inhabitants may know
"That there's a God, who governs all below:
"This great assembly too shall witness stand,
"That needs nor sword, nor spear, th' Almighty's hand:
"The battle's his, the conquest he bestows,
"And to our pow'r consigns our hated foes."
    Thus David spoke; Goliath heard and came
To meet the hero in the field of fame.
Ah ! fatal meeting to thy troops and thee,
But thou wast deaf to the divine decree :
Young David meets thee, meets thee not in vain;
'Tis thine to perish on th' ensanguin'd plain.
    And now the youth the forceful pebble flung,
Philistia trembled as it whizz'd along :
In his dread forehead, where the helmet ends,
Just o'er the brows the well-aim'd stone descends,
It pierc'd the skull, and shatter'd all the brain,
Prone on his face he tumbled to the plain :
Goliath's fall no smaller terror yields
Than riving thunders in aerial fields :
The soul still ling'red in its lov'd abode,
Till conq'ring David o'er the giant strode :
Goliath's sword then laid its master dead,
And from the body hew'd the ghastly head;
The blood in gushing torrents drench'd the plains,
The soul found passage through the spouting veins.
    And now aloud the illustrious victor said,
"Where are your boastings now your champion's dead?"

Scarce had he spoke when the Philistines fled :
But fled in vain ; the conqu'ror swift pursu'd :
What scenes of slaughter ! and what seas of blood !
"There, Saul, thy thousands grasp'd th' impurpled sand
"In pangs of death the conquest of thine hand;
"And, David, there were thy ten thousands laid:"
Thus Israel's damsels musically play'd.
    Near Gath and Ekron many an hero lay,
Breath'd out their souls, and curs'd the light of day;
Their fury quench'd by death, no longer burns,
And David with Goliath's head returns,
To Salem brought, but in his tent he plac'd
The load of armour which the giant grac'd.
His monarch saw him coming from the war,
And thus demanded of the son of Ner :
"Say, who is this amazing youth ?" he cry'd,
When thus the leader of the host reply'd :
"As lives thy soul I know not whence he sprung,
"So great in prowess though in years so young. "
"Inquire whose son is he," the sov'reign said,
"Before whose conq'ring arm Philistia fled."
Before the king behold the stripling stand,
Goliath's head depending from his hand :
To him the king :   "Say, of what martial line
"Art thou, young hero, and what sire was thine ?"
He humbly thus :   "The son of Jesse I :
"I came the glories of the field to try,
"Small is my tribe, but valiant in the fight;
"Small is my city, but thy royal right."

"Then take the promis'd gifts," the monarch cry'd,
Conferring riches and the royal bride ;
"Knit to my soul, forever thou remain
"With me, nor quit my regal roof again."

Thoughts on the Works of Providence.

ARISE, my soul, on wings enraptur'd, rise
    To praise the monarch of the earth and skies,
      Whose goodness and beneficence appear
As round its center moves the rolling year,
Or when the morning glows with rosy charms,
Or the sun slumbers in the ocean's arms,
Of light divine be a rich portion lent
To guide my soul, and favour my intent.
Celestial muse, my arduous flight sustain,
And raise my mind to a seraphic strain !
    Ador'd forever be the God unseen,
Which round the sun revolves this vast machine,
Though to his eye its mass a point appears :
Ador'd the God that whirls surrounding spheres,
Which first ordain'd that mighty Sol should reign
The peerless monarch of th' ethereal train;
Of miles twice forty millions in his height,
And yet his radiance dazzles mortal sight
So far beneath—from him th' extended earth
Vigor derives, and ev'ry flow'ry birth:
Vast through her orb she moves with easy grace
Around her Phoebus in unbounded space;

True to her course th' impetuous storm derides,
Triumphant o'er the winds and surging tides. ·
   Almighty, in these wond'rous works of thine,
What Pow'r, what Wisdom, and what Goodness shine?
And are thy wonders, Lord, by men explor'd,
And yet creating glory unador'd!
   Creation smiles in various beauty gay,
While day to night and night succeeds to day;
That Wisdom which attends Jehovah's ways,
Shines most conspicuous in the solar rays;
Without them, destitute of heat and light,
This world would be the reign of endless night;
In their excess how would our race complain,
Abhoring life! how hate its length'ned chain!
From air adust what num'rous ills would rise!
What dire contagion taint the burning skies;
What pestilential vapours, fraught with death,
Would rise, and overspread the lands beneath!
   Hail, smiling morn, that from the Orient main
Ascending dost adorn the heav'nly plain!
So rich, so various are thy beauteous dies,
That spread through all the circuit of the skies,
That, full of thee, my soul in rapture soars,
And thy great God, the cause of all adores.
   O'er beings infinite his love extends,
His wisdom rules them, and his Pow'r defends.
When tasks diurnal tire the human frame,
The spirit's faint, and dim the vital flame,
Then too that ever active bounty shines,
Which not infinity of space confines.

The sable veil, that Night in silence draws,
Conceals effects, but shows th' Almighty Cause ;
Night seals in sleep the wide creation fair,
And all is peaceful but the brow of care.
Again, gay Phoebus, as the day before,
Wakes ev'ry eye, but what shall wake no more;
Again the face of nature is renew'd,
Which still appears harmonious, fair, and good.
May grateful strains salute the smiling morn,
Before its beams the eastern hill adorn !

   Shall day to day, and night to night, conspire
To show the goodness of the Almighty Sire ?
This mental voice shall man regardless hear,
And never, never raise the filial pray'r ?
To-day, O hearken, nor your folly mourn
For time misspent, that never will return.

   But see the sons of vegetation rise,
And spread their leafy banners to the skies.
All-wise Almighty Providence do ye trace
In trees, and plants, and all the flow'ry race;
As clear as in the nobler frame of man,
All lovely copies of the Maker's plan.
The pow'r the same that forms a ray of light,
That call'd creation from eternal night.
"Let there be light," he said; from his profound
Old Chaos heard, and trembled at the sound :
Swift as the word, inspir'd by pow'r divine,
Behold the light around its Maker shine,
The first fair product of th' omnific God
And now through all his works diffus'd abroad.

As reason's pow'rs by day our God disclose,
So we may trace him in the night's repose :
Say what is sleep ? and dreams how passing strange !
When action ceases, and ideas range
Licentious and unbounded o'er the plains,
Where Fancy's queen in giddy triumph reigns,
Hear in soft strains the dreaming lover sigh
To a kind fair, or rave in jealousy;
On pleasure now, and now on vengeance bent,
The lab'ring passions struggle for a vent.
What pow'r, O man ! thy reason then restores,
So long suspended in nocturnal hours ?
What secret hand returns the mental train,
And gives improv'd thine active pow'rs again ?
From thee, O man, what gratitude should rise
And, when from balmy sleep thou op'st thine eyes,
Let thy first thoughts be praises to the skies.
How merciful our God who thus imparts
O'erflowing tides of joy to human hearts,
When wants and woes might be our righteous lot,
Our God forgetting, by our God forgot !
    Among the mental pow'rs a question rose,
"What most the image of th' Eternal shows ?"
When thus to Reason (so let Fancy rove)
Her great companion spoke immortal Love :
    "Say, mighty pow'r, how long shall strife prevail,
"And with its murmurs load the whisp'ring gale ?
"Refer the cause to Recollection's shrine,
"Who loud proclaims my origin divine,

"The cause whence heav'n and earth began to be,
"And is not man immortaliz'd by me?
"Reason, let this most causeless strife subside."
  Thus Love pronounc'd, and Reason thus repli'd:
  "Thy birth, celestial queen! 'tis mine to own,
"In thee resplendent is the Godhead shown;
"Thy words persuade, my soul enraptur'd feels
"Resistless beauty which thy smile reveals."
Ardent she spoke, and, kindling at her charms,
She clasp'd the blooming goddess in her arms.
  Infinite Love where'er we turn our eyes
Appears: this ev'ry creature's wants supplies;
This most is heard in Nature's constant voice,
This makes the morn, and this the eve rejoice;
This bids the fost'ring rains and dews descend
To nourish all, to serve one gen'ral end,
The good of man: yet man ungrateful pays
But little homage, and but little praise.
To him, whose works array'd with mercy shine,
What songs should rise, how constant, how divine!

To a Lady on the Death of Three Relations.

WE trace the pow'r of death from tomb to tomb,
    And his are all the ages yet to come.
    'Tis his to call the planets from on high,
To blacken Phoebus, and dissolve the skies;
His, too, when all in his dark realms are hurl'd,
From its firm base to shake the solid world;

His fatal sceptre rules the spacious whole,
And trembling nature rocks from pole to pole.
　　Awful he moves, and wide his wings are spread :
Behold thy brother number'd with the dead !
From bondage freed, the exulting spirit flies
Beyond Olympus, and these starry skies.
Lost in our woe for thee, blest shade, we mourn
In vain; to earth thou never must return.
Thy sisters, too, fair mourner, feel the dart
Of Death, and with fresh torture rend thine heart.
Weep not for them, who with thine happy mind
Do rise with them, and leave the world behind.
　　As a young plant by hurricanes uptorn,
So near its parent lies the newly born—
But 'midst the bright ethereal train behold
It shines superior on a throne of gold :
Then, mourner, cease; let hope thy tears restrain,
Smile on the tomb, and soothe the raging pain.
On yon blest regions fix thy longing view,
Mindless of sublunary scenes below;
Ascend the sacred mount, in thought arise,
And seek substantial and immortal joys;
Where hope revives, where faith to vision springs,
And raptur'd seraphs tune th' immortal strings
To strains ecstatic.　Thou the chorus join,
And to thy Father tune the praise divine.

To a Clergyman on the Death of His Lady.

WHEN contemplation finds her sacred spring,
    Where heav'nly music makes the arches ring,
    Where wisdom's throned, and all the graces shine,
There sits thy spouse amidst the radiant throng
    Where Virtue reigns unsulli'd and divine,
There choirs angelic shout her welcome round,
With perfect bliss and peerless glory crown'd.
While thy dear mate to flesh no more confin'd,
Exults a blest, an heav'n ascended mind,
Say in thy breast shall floods of sorrow rise?
Say shall its torrents overwhelm thine eyes?
Amid the seats of heav'n a place is free.
And angels open their bright ranks for thee;
For thee they wait and with expectant eye
Thy spouse leans downward from th' empyreal sky:
"O come away," her longing spirit cries,
"And share with me the raptures of the skies.
"Our bliss divine to mortals is unknown;
"Immortal life and glory are our own.
"There, too, may the dear pledges of our love
"Arrive, and taste with us the joys above;
"Attune the harp to more than mortal lays,
"And join with us the tribute of their praise
"To him, who dy'd stern justice to atone,
"And make eternal glory all our own.
"He in his death slew ours, and, as he rose,
"He crush'd the dire dominion of our foes;
"Vain were their hopes to put the God to flight,

"Chain us to hell, and bar the gates of light."
   She spoke and turn'd from mortal scenes her eyes,
Which beamed celestial radiance o'er the skies.
   Then thou, dear man, no more with grief retire,
Let grief no longer damp devotion's fire,
But rise sublime, to equal bliss aspire,
Thy sighs no more be wafted by the wind
No more complain, but be to heav'n resign'd,
'Twas thine t' unfold the oracles divine,
To soothe our woes the task was also thine;
Now sorrow is incumbent on thy heart,
Permit the muse a cordial to impart;
Who can to thee their tend'rest aid refuse?
To dry thy tears how longs the heav'nly muse!

———

An Hymn to the Morning.

ATTEND my lays, ye ever honour'd nine,
   Assist my labours, and my strains refine;
      In smoothest numbers pour the notes along,
For bright Aurora now demands my song.
   Aurora, hail, and all the thousand dyes,
Which deck thy progress through the vaulted skies;
The morn awakes, and wide extends her rays,
On ev'ry leaf the gentle zephyr plays;
Harmonious lays the feather'd race resume,
Dart the bright eye, and shake the painted plume.
   Ye shady groves, your verdant gloom display
To shield your poet from the burning day:

Calliope, awake the sacred lyre,
While thy fair sisters fan the pleasing fire :
The bow'rs, the gales, the variegated skies
In all their pleasures in my bosom rise.
    See in the east th' illustrious king of day !
His rising radiance drives the shades away—
But oh ! I feel his fervid leaves too strong,
And scarce begun, concludes th' abortive song.

An Hymn to the Evening.

SOON as the sun forsook the eastern main
    The pealing thunder shook the heav'nly plain ;
    Majestic grandeur ! From the zephyr's wing,
Exhales the incense of the blooming spring,
Soft purl the streams, the birds renew their notes,
And through the air their mingled music floats.
Through all the heav'ns what beauteous dyes are spread!
But the west glories in the deepest red :
So may our breasts with every virtue glow,
The living temples of our God below !
    Fill'd with the praise of him who gives the light,
And draws the sable curtains of the night,
Let placid slumbers soothe each weary mind,
At morn to wake more heav'nly, more refin'd;
So shall the labors of the day begin
More pure, more guarded from the snares of sin.
    Night's leaden sceptre seals my drowsy eyes,
Then cease, my song, till fair Aurora rise.

Isaiah LXIII, 1-8

SAY, heav'nly muse, what king, or mighty God,
That moves sublime from Idumea's road?
In Bozrah's dies, with martial glories join'd
His purple vesture waves upon the wind.
Why thus enrob'd delights he to appear
In the dread image of the Pow'r of war?
Compress'd in wrath the swelling wine-press groaned,
It bled, and pour'd the gushing purple round.
"Mine was the act," th' Almighty Saviour said,
And shook the dazzling glories of his head.
"When all forsook I trod the press alone,
"And conquer'd by omnipotence of my own;
"For man's release sustained the pond'rous load,
"For man the wrath of an immortal God :
"To execute th' Eternal's dread command
"My soul I sacrific'd with willing hand;
"Sinless I stood before the avenging frown,
"Atoning thus for vices not my own."
His eye the ample field of battle round
Survey'd, but no created succours found;
His own omnipotence sustain'd the fight,
His vengeance sunk the haughty foes in night;
Beneath his feet the prostrate troops were spread,
And round him lay the dying, and the dead.
Great God, what lightn'ing flashes from thine eyes?
What pow'r withstands if thou indignant rise?
Against thy Zion though her foes may rage,
And their cunning, all their strength engage,
Yet she serenely on thy bosom lies,
Smiles at their arts, and all their force defies.

On Recollection.

MNEME, begin. Inspire, ye sacred nine,
Your vent'rous Afric in her great design.
Mneme, immortal pow'r, I trace thy spring :
Assist my strains, while I thy glories sing :
The acts of long departed years, by thee
Recover'd, in due order rang'd we see :
Thy pow'r the long-forgotten calls from night,
That sweetly plays before the fancy's sight.
  Mneme in our nocturnal vision pours
The ample treasure of her secret stores;
Swift from above she wings her silent flight
Through Phœbe's realms, fair regent of the night;
And, in her pomp of images display'd,
To the high-raptur'd poet gives her aid,
Through the unbounded regions of the mind,
Diffusing light celestial andrefin'd.
The heav'nly phantom paints the actions done
By ev'ry tribe beneath the rolling sun.
  Mneme, enthron'd within the human breast,
Has vice condemn'd and ev'ry virtue blest.
How sweet the sound when we her plaudits hear !
Sweeter than music to the ravish'd ear,
Sweeter than Maro's entertaining strains
Resounding through the groves, and hills, and plains.
But how is Mneme dreaded by the race,
Who scorn her warnings and despise her grace !
By her unveil'd each horrid crime appears,
Her awful hand a cup of wormwood bears.

Days, years misspent, O what a hell of woe !
Her's the worst tortures that our souls can know.
  Now eighteen years their destin'd course have run
In fast succession round the central sun.
How did the follies of that period pass
Unnotic'd, but hehold them writ in brass !
In Recollection see them fresh return,
And sure 'tis mine to be asham'd, and mourn.
  O Virtue, smiling in immortal green,
Do thou exert thy pow'r, and change the scene;
Be thine employ to guide my future days,
And mine to pay the tribute of my praise,
  Of Recollection such the pow'r enthron'd
In every breast, and thus her pow'r is own'd.
The wretch, who dar'd the vengeance of the skies,
At last awakes in horror and surprise,
By her alarm'd, he sees impending fate,
He howls in anguish and repents too late.
But O ! what peace, what joys are her's t' impart
To ev'ry holy, ev'ry upright heart !
Thrice blest the man, who in her sacred shrine,
Feels himself shelter'd from the wrath divine !

On Imagination.

THY various works, imperial queen, we see,
    How bright their forms! how deck'd with pomp by thee!
    Thy wond'rous acts in beauteous order stand,
And all attest how potent is thine hand.
    From Helicon's refulgent heights attend
Ye sacred choir; and my attempts befriend:
To tell her glories with a faithful tongue,
Ye blooming graces, triumph in my song.
    Now here, now there; the roving Fancy flies,
Till some lov'd object strikes her wand'ring eyes.
Whose silken fetters all the senses bind,
And soft captivity involves the mind.
    Imagination! who can sing thy force?
Or who describe the swiftness of thy course?
Soaring through air to find the bright abode,
Th' empyreal palace of the thund'ring God,
We on thy pinions can surpass the wind,
And leave the rolling universe behind:
From star to star the mental optics rove,
Measure the skies, and range the realms above.
There in one view we grasp the mighty whole,
Or with new worlds amaze th' unbounded soul.
    Though winter frowns to Fancy's raptur'd eyes
The fields may flourish, and gay scenes arise;
The frozen deeps may break their iron bands,
And bid their waters murmur o'er the sands.
Fair Flora may resume her fragrant reign,
And with her flow'ry riches deck the plain;

Sylvanus may diffuse his honors round,
And all the forest may with leaves be crown'd :
Show'rs may descend, and dews their gems disclose
And nectar sparkle on the blooming rose.

   Such is thy pow'r, nor are thine orders vain,
O thou the leader of the mental train :
In full perfection all thy works are wrought,
And thine the sceptre o'er the realms of thought.
Before thy throne the subject-passions bow,
Of subject-passions sov'reign ruler thou;
At thy command joy rushes on the heart,
And through the glowing veins the spirits dart.
Fancy might now her silken pinions try
To rise from earth, and sweep th' expanse on high;
From Tithon's bed now might Aurora rise,
Her cheeks all glowing with celestial dies,
While a pure stream of light o'erflows the skies,
The monarch of the day I might behold,
And all the mountains tipt with radiant gold.
But I reluctant leave the pleasing views,
Which Fancy dresses to delight the Muse;
Winter austere forbids me to aspire,
And northern tempests damp the rising fire;
They chill the tides of Fancy's flowing sea,
Cease then, my song, cease the unequal lay.

A Funeral Poem on the Death of C. E., An Infant of Twelve Months.

THROUGH airy roads he wings his infant flight
    To purer regions of celestial light;
      Enlarg'd he sees unnumber'd systems roll,
Beneath him sees the universal whole,
Planets on planets run their destin'd roumd,
And circling wonders fill the vast profound,
Th' ethereal now, and now th' empyreal skies
With growing splendors strike his wond'ring eyes:
The angels view him with delight unknown,
Press his soft hand, and seat him on his throne;
Then smiling thus : "To this divine abode,
"The seat of saints, of seraphs, and of God,
"Thrice welcome thou." The raptur'd babe replies,
"Thanks to my God, who snatch'd me to the skies;
"E'er vice triumphant had possess'd my heart,
"E'er yet the tempter had beguil'd my heart,
"E'er yet on sin's base actions I was bent,
"E'er yet I knew temptation's dire intent ;
"E'er yet the lash for horrid crimes I felt,
"E'er vanity had led my way to guilt;
"But, soon arriv'd at my celestial goal
"Full glories rush on my expanding soul."
Joyful he spoke : Exulting cherubs round
Clapt their glad wings, the heav'nly vaults resound.
  Say, parents, why this unavailing moan ?
Why heave your pensive bosoms with the groan ?

To Charles, the happy subject of my song,
A brighter world, and nobler strains belong.
Say would you tear him from the realms above
By thoughtless wishes, and prepost'rous love?
Doth his felicity increase your pain?
Or could you welcome to this world again
This heir of bliss? With a superior air
Methinks he answers with a smile severe,
"Thrones and dominions cannot tempt me there."
But still you cry, "Can we the sigh forbear,
"And still and still must we not pour the tear?
"Our only hope, more dear than vital breath,
"Twelve moons revolv'd, becomes the prey of death;
"Delightful infant, nightly visions give
"Thee to our arms, and we with joy receive,
"We fain would clasp the Phantom to our breast,
"The Phantom flies and leaves the soul unblest."
    To yon bright regions let your faith ascend,
Prepare to join your dearest infant friend
In pleasures without measure, without end.

To Captain H——d, of the 65th Regiment.

SAY, muse divine, can hostile scenes delight
    The warrior's bosom in the fields of fight?
        Lo ! here the Christian and the hero join
With mutual grace to form the man divine.
In H-——d, see with pleasure and surprise,
Where valour kindles, and where virtue lies :
Go, hero brave, still grace the post of fame,
And add new glories to thine honour'd name,
Still to the field, and still to virtue true :
Britannia glories in no son like you.

To the Right Honorable William, Earl of Dartmouth, His Majesty's Secretary of State for North America, Etc.

HAIL, happy day, when, smiling like the morn,
    Fair Freedom rose New-England to adorn :
        The northern clime beneath her genial ray,
Dartmouth, congratulates thy blissful sway :
Elate with hope her race no longer mourns,
Each soul expands, each grateful bosom burns,
While in thine hand with pleasure we behold
The silken reins, and Freedom's charms unfold.
Long lost to realms beneath the northern skies
She shines supreme, while hated faction dies :
Soon as appear'd the Goddess long desir'd,
Sick as the view, she languish'd and expir'd ;
Thus from the splendors of the morning light
The owl in sadness seeks the caves of night.

No more America in mournful strain
Of wrongs, and grievance unredress'd complain,
No longer shalt thou dread the iron chain,
Which wanton Tyranny with lawless hand
Had made, and which it meant t' enslave the land.
  Should you, my lord, while you peruse my song,
Wonder from whence my love of Freedom sprung,
Whence flow these wishes for the common good,
By feeling hearts alone best understood,
I, young in life, by seeming cruel fate
Was snatch'd from Afric's fancy'd happy seat :
What pangs excruciating must molest,
What sorrows labour in my parent's breast !
Steel'd was the soul and by no misery mov'd
That from a father seiz'd his babe belov'd.
Such, such my case.   And can I then but pray
Others may never feel tyrannic sway ?
    For favours past, great Sir, our thanks are due,
And thee we ask thy favours to renew,
Since in thy pow'r, as in thy will before,
To sooth the griefs, which thou did'st once deplore.
May heav'nly grace the sacred sanction give
To all thy works, and thou for ever live
Not only on the wings of fleeting Fame,
Though praise immortal crowns the patriot's name,
But to conduct to heav'n's refulgent fane,
May fiery courses sweep th' ethereal plain,
And bear thee upwards to that blest abode,
Where, like prophet, thou shalt find thy God.

Ode to Neptune.

On Mrs. W——'s Voyage to England.

I

WHILE raging tempests shake the shore,
　　While Æ'lus' thunders round us roar,
　　And sweep impetuous o'er the plain
Be still, O tyrant of the main;
Nor let thy brow contracted frowns betray,
While my Susannah skims the wat'ry way.

II

The Pow'r propitious hears the lay,
The blue-ey'd daughters of the sea
With sweeter cadence glide along,
And Thames responsive joins their song.
Pleas'd with their notes Sol sheds benign his ray,
And double radiance decks the face of day.

III

To Court thee to Britannia's arms
　　Serene the climes and mild the sky,
Her region boasts unnumber'd charms,
　　Thy welcome smiles in ev'ry eye.
Thy promise, Neptune, keep, record my pray'r,
Nor give my wishes to the empty air.

　　　　　　　　Boston, October 10, 1772.

To a Lady on Her Coming to North America
With Her Son, for the Recovery
of Her Health.

INDULGENT muse ! my grov'ling mind inspire,
    And fill my bosom with celestial fire.
        See from Jamaica's fervid shore she moves,
Like the fair mother of the blooming loves,
When from above the Goddess with her hand
Fans the soft breeze, and lights upon the land;
Thus she on Neptune's wat'ry realm reclin'd
Appear'd, and thus invites the ling'ring wind.
    "Arise, ye winds, America explore,
"Waft me, ye gales, from this malignant shore;
"The Northern milder climes I long to greet,
"There hope that health will my arrival meet."
Soon as she spoke in my ideal view
The winds assented, and the vessel flew.
    Madam, your spouse bereft of wife and son,
In the grove's dark recesses pours his moan;
Each branch, wide-spreading to the ambient sky,
Forgets its verdue, and submits to die.
    From thence I turn, and leave the sultry plain,
And swift pursue thy passage o'er the main :
The ship arrives before the fav'ring wind,
And makes the Philadelphian port assign'd,
Thence I attend you to Bostonia's arms,
Where gen'rous friendship ev'ry bosom warms :
Thrice welcome here !   may health revive again,
Bloom on thy cheek, and bound in ev'ry vein !

Then back return to gladden ev'ry heart,
And give your spouse his soul's far dearer part,
Receiv'd again with what a sweet surprise,
The tear in transport starting from his eyes !
While his attendant son with blooming grace
Springs to his father's ever dear embrace.
With shouts of joy Jamaica's rocks resound,
With shouts of joy the country rings around.

To a Lady on Her Remarkable Preservation in a Hurricane in North Carolina.

THOUGH thou did'st hear the tempest from afar,
    And felt'st the horrors of the wat'ry war,
        To me unknown, yet on this peaceful shore
Methinks I hear the storm tumultuous roar,
And how stern Boreas with impetuous hand
Compell'd the Nereids to usurp the land.
Reluctant rose the daughters of the main,
And slow ascending glided o'er the plain,
Till Æolus in his rapid chariot drove
In gloomy grandeur from the vault above :
Furious he comes. His winged sons obey
Their frantic sire, and madden all the sea.
The billows rave, the wind's fierce tyrant roars,
And with his thrund'ring terrors shakes the shores :
Broken by waves the vessel's frame is rent,
And strows with planks the wat'ry element.

But thee, Maria, a kind Nereid's shield
Preserv'd from sinking, and thy form upheld :
And sure some heav'nly oracle design'd
At that dread crisis to instruct thy mind
Things of eternal consequence to weigh,
And to thine heart just feelings to convey
Of things above, and of the future doom,
And what the births of the dread world to come.
    From tossing seas I welcome thee to land.
"Resign her, Nereid," 'twas thy God's command.
Thy spouse late buried, as thy fears conceiv'd,
Again returns, thy fears are all reliev'd :
Thy daughter blooming with superior grace
Again thou see'st, again thine arms embrace ;
O come, and joyful show thy spouse his heir,
And what the blessings of maternal care !

———

To a Lady and Her Children, on the Death of Her Son and Their Brother.

O'ERWHELMING sorrow now demands my song :
    From death the overwhelming sorrow sprung.
    What flowing tears ! What hearts with grief oppres't !
What sighs on sighs heave the fond parent's breast !
The brother weeps, the hapless sisters join
Th' increasing woe, and swell the crystal brine;
The poor, who once his gen'rous bounty fed,
Droop, and bewail their benefactor dead.

In death the friend, the kind companion lies,
And in one death what various comfort dies !
   Th' unhappy mother sees the sanguine rill
Forget to flow, and nature's wheels stand still,
But see from earth his spirit far remov'd,
And know no grief recalls your best-belov'd:
He, upon pinions swifter than the wind,
Has left mortality's sad scenes behind
For joys to this terrestrial state unknown,
And glories richer than the monarch's crown.
Of virtue's steady course the prize behold !
What blissful wonders to his mind unfold
But of celestial joys I sing in vain :
Attempt not, muse, the too advent'rous strain.
   No more in briny show'rs, ye friends around,
Or bathe his clay, or waste them on the ground :
Still do you weep, still wish for his return ?
How cruel thus to wish, and thus to mourn !
No more for him the streams of sorrow pour,
But has to join him on the heav'nly shore,
On harps of gold to tune immortal lays,
And to your God immortal anthems raise.

To a Gentleman and Lady on the Death of the Lady's Brother and Sister, and a Child of the Name of Avis, Aged One Year.

ON death's domain intent I fix my eyes,
    Where human nature in vast ruin lies :
    With pensive mind I search the drear abode,
Where the great conqu'or has his spoils bestow'd ;
There the offspring of six thousand years
In endless numbers to my view appears :
Whole kingdoms in his gloomy den are thrust,
And nations ix with their primeval dust :
Insatiate still he gluts the ample tomb ;
His is the present, his the age to come.
See here a brother, here a sister spread,
And a sweet daughter mingled with the dead.

    But, Madam, let your grief be laid aside,
And let the fountain of your tears be dry'd,
In vain they flow to wet the dusty plain,
Your sighs are wafted to the skies in vain,
Your pains they witness, but they can no more,
While death reigns tyrant o'er this mortal shore.

    The glowing stars and silver queen of light
At last must perish in the gloom of night :
Resign thy friends to that Almighty hand,
Which gave them life, and bow to his command :
Thine Avis give without a murm'ring heart,
Though half thy soul be fated to depart.
To shining guards consign thine infant care
To waft triumphant through the seats of air :

Her soul enlarg'd to heav'nly pleasure springs,
She feeds on truth and uncreated things.
Methinks I hear her in the realms above,
And leaning forward with a filial love,
Invite you there to share immortal bliss
Unknown, untasted in a state like this.
With tow'ring hopes, and growing grace arise,
And seek beatitude beyond the skies.

On the Death of Dr. Samuel Marshall, 1771.

THROUGH thickest glooms look back, immortal shade,
    On that confusion which thy death has made;
    Or from Olympus' height look down, and see
A town involv'd in grief bereft of thee.
Thy Lucy sees thee mingle with the dead,
And rends the graceful tresses from her head,
Wild in her woe, with grief unknown opprest
Sigh follows sigh deep heaving from her breast.
    Too quickly fled, ah! whither art thou gone?
Ah! lost for ever to thy wife and son!
The hapless child, thine only hope and heir,
Clings round his mother's neck and weeps his sorrows there.
The loss of thee on Tyler's soul returns,
And Boston for her dear physician mourns.
    When sickness call'd for Marshall's healing hand,
With what compassion did his soul expand?
In him we found the father and the friend:
In life how lov'd! how honour'd in his end!

And must not then our Æsculapius stay
To bring his ling'ring infant into day?
The babe unborn in the dark womb is tost,
And seems in anguish for its father lost.
    Gone is Apollo from his house of earth,
But leaves the sweet memorials of his worth:
The common parent, whom we all deplore,
From yonder world unseen must come no more,
Yet 'midst our woes immortal hopes attend
The spouse, the sire, the universal friend.

To a Gentleman on His Voyage to Great Britain for the Recovery of His Health.

WHILE others chant of gay Elysian scenes,
    Of balmy zephyrs, and of flow'ry plains,
        My song more happy speaks a greater name,
Feels higher motives and a nobler flame.
For thee, O R——, the muse attunes her strings,
And mounts sublime above inferior things.
    I sing not now of green embow'ring woods,
I sing not now the daughters of the floods,
I sing not of the storms o'er ocean driv'n,
And how they howl'd along the waste of heav'n,
But I to R—— would paint the British shore,
And vast Atlantic, not untry'd before:
Thy life impair'd commands thee to arise,
Leave these bleak regions and inclement skies,
Where chilling winds return the winter past,
And nature shudders at the furious blast.

O thou stupenduous, earth-enclosing main
Exert thy wonders to the world again !
If ere thy pow'r prolong'd the fleeting breath,
Turn'd back the shafts, and mock'd the gates of death,
If ere thine air dispens'd an healing pow'r,
Or snatch'd the victim from the fatal hour,
This equal case demands thine equal care,
And equal wonders may this patient share.
But unavailing, frantic is the dream
To hope thine aid without the aid of him
Who gave thee birth and taught thee where to flow,
And in thy waves his various blessings show.
　　May R—— return to view his native shore,
Replete with vigour not his own before.
Then shall we see with pleasure and surprise,
And own thy work, great Ruler of the skies !

To the Rev. Dr. Thomas Amory, on Reading His Sermons on Daily Devotion, in Which that Duty is Recommended and Assisted.

TO cultivate in ev'ry noble mind
　　Habitual grace, and sentiments refin'd,
　　Thus while you strive to mend the human heart,
Thus while the heav'nly precepts you impart,
O may each bosom catch the sacred fire,
And youthful minds to Virtue's throne aspire !
　　When God's eternal ways you set in sight
And Virtue shines in all her native light,

In vain would Vice her works in night conceal,
For Wisdom's eye pervades the sable veil.

Artists may paint the sun's effulgent rays,
But Amory's pen the brighter God displays;
While his great works in Amory's pages shine,
And while he proves his essence all divine,
The Athiest sure no more can boast aloud
Of chance, or nature, and exclude the God;
As if the clay without the potter's aid
Should rise in various forms, and shapes self-made,
Or worlds above with orb o'er orb profound
Self-mov'd could run the everlasting round.
It cannot be—unerring Wisdom guides
With eye propitious, and o'er all presides.

Still prosper, Amory! still may'st thou receive
The warmest blessings that a muse can give,
And when this transitory fate is o'er,
When kingdoms fall, and fleeting Fame's no more,
May Amory triumph in immortal fame,
A nobler title, and superior name!

On the Death of J. C., An Infant.

NO more the flow'ry scenes of pleasure rise,
　　Nor charming prospects greet the mental eyes,
　　No more with joy we view that lovely face
Smiling, disportive, flush'd with ev'ry grace.

　　The tear of sorrow flows from ev'ry eye,
Groans answer groans, and sighs to sighs reply;
What sudden pangs shot thro' each aching heart,
When, Death, thy messenger dispatch'd his dart?
Thy dread attendants, all-destroying Pow'r,
Hurried the infant to his mortal hour.
Could'st thou unpitying close those radiant eyes?
Or fail'd his artless beauties to surprise?
Could not his innocence thy stroke controul
Thy purpose shake, and soften all thy soul?

　　The blooming babe, with shades of death o'er-spread
No more shall smile, no more shall raise its head,
But, like a branch, that from the tree is torn,
Falls prostrate, wither'd, languid, and forlorn,
"Where flies my James?"　'Tis thus I seem to hear
The parent ask, "Some angel tell me where
"He wings his passage thro' the yielding air?"
Methinks a cherub bending from the skies
Observes the question, and serene replies,
"In heav'n's high places your babe appears:
"Prepare to meet him, and dismiss your tears."
Shall not th' intelligence your grief restrain,
And turn the mournful to the cheerful strain?

Cease your complaints, suspend each rising sigh,
Cease to accuse the Ruler of the sky.
Parents, no more indulge the falling tear :
Let faith to heav'n's refulgent domes repair,
There see your infant, like a seraph glow :
What charms celestial in his numbers flow
Melodious, while the soul-enchanting strain
Dwells on his tongue, and fills th' ethereal plain ?
Enough—forever cease your murm'ring breath;
Not as a foe, but friend converse with Death,
Since to the port of happiness unknown
He brought that treasure which you call your own.
The gift of heav'n intrusted to your hand
Cheerful resign at the divine command:
Not at your bar must sov'reign Wisdom stand.

An Hymn to Humanity.

To S. P. C., Esq.

I.

LO ! for this dark terrestrial ball
   Forsakes his azure-paved hall
    A prince of heav'nly birth !
Divine Humanity behold,
What wonders rise, what charms unfold
    At his descent to earth !

II.

The bosoms of the great and good
With wonder and delight he view'd,
    And fix'd his empire there:
Him, close compressing to his breast,
The sire of gods and men address'd,
    "My son, my heav'nly fair !

III.

" Descend to earth, there place thy throne;
" To succor man's afflicted son
   " Each human heart inspire:
" To act in bounties unconfin'd
" Enlarge the close contracted mind,
   " And fill it with thy fire."

93

IV.

Quick as the word, with swift career
He wings his course from star to star,
  And leaves the bright abode.
The Virtue did his charms impart;
Their G——! then thy raptur'd heart
  Perceived the rushing God:

V.

For when thy pitying eye did see
The languid muse in low degree,
  Then, then at thy desire
Descended the celestial nine;
O'er me methougt they deign'd to shine,
  And deign'd to string my lyre.

VI.

Can Afric's muse forgetful prove?
Or can such friendship fail to move
  A tender human heart?
Immortal Friendship laurel-crown'd
The smiling Graces all surround
  With ev'ry heav'nly Art.

To the Honorable T. H., Esq., on the Death of His Daughter

WHILE deep you mourn beneath the cypress-shade
The hand of Death, and your dear daughter laid
In dust, whose absence gives your tears to flow,
And racks your bosom with incessant woe,
Let Recollection take a tender part,
Assuage the raging tortures of your heart,
Still the wild tempest of tumultuous grief,
And pour the heav'nly nectar of relief:
Suspend the sigh, dear Sir, and check the groan,
Divinely bright your daughter's Virtues shone:
How free from scornful pride her gentle mind,
Which ne'er its aid to indigence declin'd!
Expanding free, it sought the means to prove
Unfailing charity, unbounded love!
    She unreluctant flies to see no more
Her dear-lov'd parents on earth's dusky shore:
Impatient heav'n's resplendent goal to gain,
She with swift progress cuts the azure plain,
Where grief subsides, where changes are no more,
And life's tumultuous billows cease to roar;
She leaves her earthly mansion for the skies,
Where new creations feast her wond'ring eyes.
    To heav'n's high mandate cheerfully resign'd
She mounts, and leaves the rolling globe behind;
She, who late wish'd Leonard might return,
Has ceas'd to languish, and forgot to mourn;
To the same high empyreal mansions come,
She joins her spouse, and smiles upon the tomb:

And thus I hear her from the realms above:
" Lo I this the kingdom of celestial love !
" Could ye, fond parents, see our present bliss,
" How soon would you each sigh, each fear dismiss ?
" Amidst unutter'd pleasures whilst I play
" In the fair sunshine of celestial day,
" As far as grief affects an happy soul
" So far doth grief my better mind controul,
" To see on earth my aged parents mourn,
" And secret wish for T——l to return:
" Let brighter scenes your ev'ning hours employ:
" Converse with heav'n, and taste the promis'd joy.

Niobe in Distress for Her Children Slain by Apollo, From Ovid's Metamorphoses, Book VI, and From a View of the Painting of Mr. Richard Wilson.

APOLLO'S wrath to man the dreadful spring
  Of ills innum'rous, tuneful goddess, sing !
Thou who did'st first th' ideal pencil give,
And taught'st the painter in his works to live,
Inspire with glowing energy of thought,
What Wilson painted, and Ovid wrote.
Muse ! lend thy aid, nor let me sue in vain,
Tho' last and meanest of the rhyming train !
O guide my pen in lofty strains to show
The Phrygian queen. all beautiful in woe.
  'Twas where Maeonia spreads her wide domain
Niobe dwelt, and held her potent reign :
See in her hand the regal sceptre shine,
The wealthy heir of Tantalus divine,
He most distinguish'd by Dodonean Jove,
To approach the tables of the gods above:
Her grandsire Atlas, who with mighty pains
Th' ethereal axis on his neck sustains:
Her other grandsire on the throne on high
Rolls the loud pealing thunder thro' the sky.
  Her spouse, Amphion, who from Jove, too, springs,
Divinely taught to sweep the sounding strings.
  Seven sprightly sons the royal bed adorn,
Seven daughters beauteous as the op'ning morn,
As when Aurora fills the ravish'd sight,
And decks the orient realms with rosy light

97

From their bright eyes the living splendors play,
Nor can beholders bear the flashing ray.
 Whenever, Niobe, thou turn'st thine eyes,
New beauties kindle, and new joys arise !
But thou had'st far the happier mother prov'd,
If this fair offspring had been less belov'd:
What if their charms exceed Aurora's tint.
No words could tell them, and no pencil paint,
Thy love too vehement hastens to destroy
Each blooming maid, and each celestial boy.
 Now Manto comes, endu'd with mighty skill
The past to explore, the future to reveal.
Thro' Thebes' wide streets Tiresia's daughter came,
Divine Latona's mandate to proclaim:
The Theban maids to hear the order ran,
When thus Maeonia's prophetess began:
 " Go, Thebans ! great Latona's will obey,
" And pious tribute at her altars pay:
" With rights divine, the goddess be implor'd,
" Nor be her sacred offering unador'd."
Thus Manto spoke. The Theban maids obey,
And pious tribute to the goddess pay.
The rich perfumes ascend in waving spires,
And altars blaze with consecrated fires ;
The fair assembly moves with graceful air,
And leaves of laurel bind the flowing hair.
 Niobe comes with all her royal race,
With charms unnumber'd, and superior grace :
Her Phrygian garments of delightful hue,
Inwove with gold, refulgent to the view,

Beyond description beautiful she moves
Like heav'nly Venus, 'midt her smiles and loves :
She views around the supplicating train,
And shakes her graceful head with stern disdain.
Proudly she turns around her lofty eyes,
And thus reviles celestial deities :
"What madness drives the Theban ladies fair
"To give their incense to surrounding air ?
"Say why this new sprung deity preferred ?
"Why vainly fancy your petitions heard ?
" Or say why Goen's offspring is obey'd,
" While to my goddess-ship no tribut's paid ?
" For me no altars blaze with living fires,
" No bullock bleeds, no frankincense transpires,
" Thro' Cadmus' palace, not unknown to fame,
" And Phrygian nations all revere my name.
" Where'er I turn my eyes vast wealth I find,
" Lo ! here an empress with a goddess join'd.
" What, shall a Titaness be deify'd,
" To whom the spacious earth a couch deny'd !
" Nor heav'n, nor earth, nor sea receiv'd your queen,
" Till pitying Delos took the wand'rer in.
" Round me what a large progeny is spread !
" No frowns of fortune has my soul to dread.
" What if indignant she decrease my train ?
" More than Latona's number will remain.
" Then hence, ye Theban dames, hence haste away,
" Nor longer off'rings to Latona pay !

" Regard the orders of Amphion's spouse,
" And take the leaves of laurels from your brows. "
Niobe spoke. The Theban maids obey'd,
Their brows unbound, and left the rites unpaid.
   The angry goddess heard, then silence broke
On Cynthus' summit, and indignant spoke:
" Phoebus ! behold, thy mother in disgrace,
" Who to no goddess yields the prior place
" Except to Juno's self, who reigns above,
" The spouse and sister of the thund'ring Jove.
" Niobe, sprung from Tantalus, inspires
" Each Theban bosom with rebellious fires;
" No reason her imperious temper quells,
" But all her father in her tongue rebels;
" Wrap her own sons for her blaspheming breath.
" Apollo ! wrap them in the shades of death. "
Latona ceas'd, and ardent thus replies
The God, whose glory decks th' expanded skies.
   " Cease thy complaints, mine be the task assign'd
" To punish pride, and scourge the rebel mind."
This Phœbe join'd.—They wing their instant flight;
Thebes trembled as th' immortal pow'rs alight.
   With clouds incompass'd glorious Phoebus stands;
The feather'd vengeance quiv'ring in his hands.
   Near Cadmus' walls a plain extended lay,
Where Thebus' young princes pass'd in sport the day:
There the bold coursers bounded o'er the plains,
While the great masters held the golden reins.
Ismenus first the racing pastime led,
And rul'd the fury of his flying steed.

" Ah, me," he sudden cries, with shrieking breath,
While in his breast he feels the shaft of death;
He drops the bridle on his courser's mane,
Before his eyes in shadows swims the plain,
He, the first-born of great Amphion's bed,
Was struck the first, first mingled with the dead.
 Then did'st thou, Sipylus, the language hear
Of fate portentous whistling in the air:
As when th' impending storm the sailor sees
He spreads his canvas to the fav'ring breeze.
So to thine horse thou gav'st the golden reins,
Gav'st him to rush impetuous o'er the plains:
But, ah! a fatal shaft from Phoebus' hand
Smites thro' thy neck, and sinks thee on the sand.
 Two other brothers were at wrestling found,
And in the pastime clasp each other round:
A shaft that instant from Apollo's hand
Transfixt them both, and stretch'd them on the sand:
Together they their cruel fate bemoan'd,
Toge'her languish'd, and together groan'd:
Together too th' unbodied spirits fled,
And sought the gloomy mansions of the dead.
 Alphenor saw, and trembling at the view,
Beat his torn breast, that chang'd its snowy hue.
He flies to raise them in a kind embrace;
A brother's fondness triumphs in his face:
Alphenor fails in this fraternal deed,
A dart dispatch'd him (so the fates decreed:)
Soon as the arrow left the deadly wound,
His issuing entrails smoak'd upon the ground.

What woes on blooming Damasichon wait!
His sighs portend his near impending fate.
Just where the well-made leg begins to be,
And the soft sinews form the supple knee,
The youth sore wounded by the Delian god
Attempts t' extract the crime-avenging rod,
But, whilst he strives the will of fate t' avert,
Divine Apollo sends a second dart;
Swift thro' his throat the feather'd mischief flies,
Bereft of sense, he drops his head, and dies.

Young Illioneus, the last directs his pray'r,
And cries, "My life, ye gods celestial! spare,"
Apollo heard, and pity touch'd his heart,
But ah! too late, for he had sent the dart:
Thou, too, O Illioneus, art doom'd to fall,
The fates refuse that arrow to recall.

On the swift wings of ever-flying Fame
To Cadmus' palace soon the tidings came:
Niobe heard, and with indignant eyes
She thus express'd her anger and surprise:
"Why is such privilege to them allow'd?
"Why thus insulted by the Delian god?
"Dwells there such mischief in the pow'rs above?'
"Why sweeps the vengeance of immortal Jove?"
For now Amphion too, with grief oppress'd
Had plung'd the deadly dagger in his breast.
Niobe now, less haughty than before,
With lofty head directs her steps no more.
She, who late told her pedigree divine,
And drove the Thebans from Latona's shrine,

102

How strangely chang'd !—yet beautiful in woe,
She weeps, nor weeps unpity'd by the foe.
On each pale corse the wretched mother spread
Lay overwhelm'd with grief, and kiss'd her dead,
Then rais'd her arms, and thus in accents slow,
"Be sated cruel Goddess ! with my woe ;
"If I've offended, let these streaming eyes,
"And let this sev'nfold funeral suffice :
"Ah take this wretched life you deigned to save,
"With them I too am carried to the grave.
"Rejoice triumphant, my victorious foe,
"But show the cause from whence your triumphs flow ?
"Tho' I unhappy mourn these children slain,
"Yet greater numbers to my lot remain."
She ceas'd, the bow string twang'd with awful sound,
Which struck with terror all th' assembly round,
Except the queen, who stood unmov'd alone,
By her distresses more presumptuous grown.
Near the pale corses stood their sisters fair
In sable vestures and dishevell'd hair.
One, while she draws the fatal shaft away,
Faints, falls and sickens at the light of day.
To soothe her mother, lo ! another flies,
And blames the fury of inclement skies,
And, while her words a filial pity show,
Struck dumb—indignant seeks the shades below.
Now from the fatal place another flies,
Falls in her flight, and languishes, and dies.
Another on her sister drops in death ;
A fifth in trembling terrors yields her breath ;

While the sixth seeks some gloomy cave in vain,
Struck with the rest and mingled with the slain.

One only daughter lives, and she the least ;
The queen close clasp'd the daughter to her breast :
"Ye heav'nly pow'rs, ah spare me one," she cry'd,
"Ah ! spare me one," the vocal hills reply'd :
In vain she begs, the fates her suit deny,
In her embrace she sees her daughter die.

*The queen of all her family bereft,
"Without or husband, son, or daughter left,
"Grew stupid at the shock.   The passing air
"Made no impression on her stiff'ning hair.
"The blood forsook for her face : amidst the flood
"Pour'd from her cheeks, quite fi'xd her eye-balls stood.
"Her tongue, her palate both abdurate grew,
"Her curdled veins no longer motion knew ;
"The use of neck, and arms, and feet was gone,
"And ev'n her bowels hard'ned into stone :
"A marble statue now the queen appears,
"But from the marble steal the silent tears."

*This Verse to the End is the Work of another Hand.

To S. M., a Young African Painter, on Seeing His Works.

To show the lab'ring bosom's deep intent,
And thought in living characters to paint.
When first thy pencil did those beauties give,
And breathing figures learnt from thee to live,
How did those prospects give my soul delight,
A new creation rushing on my sight?
Still, wond'rous youth! each noble path pursue,
On deathless glories fix thine ardent view:
Still may the painter's and the poet's fire
To aid thy pencil, and thy verse conspire!
And may the charms of each seraphic theme
Conduct thy footseps to immortal fame!
High to the blissful wonders of the skies
Elate thy soul, and raise thy wishful eyes.
Thrice happy, when exalted to survey
That splendid city, crown'd with endless day,
Whose twice six gates on radiant hinges ring:
Celestial Salem blooms in endless spring.
  Calm and serene thy moments glide along,
And may the muse inspire each future song!
Still, with the sweets of contemplation bless'd,
May peace with balmy wings your soul invest!
But when these shades of time are chas'd away,
And darkness ends in everlasting day,
On what seraphic pinions shall we move,
And view the landscapes in the realms above?

There shall thy tongue in heav'nly murmurs flow,
And there my muse with heav'nly transport glow:
No more to tell of Damon's tender sighs,
Or rising radiance of Aurora's eyes,
For nobler themes demand a nobler strain,
And purer language on th' ethereal plain.
Cease, gentle muse! the solemn gloom of night
Now seals the fair creation from my sight.

To His Honour the Lieutenant-Governor, on the Death of His Lady, March 24, 1773.

All-Conquering Death! by thy resistless pow'r
Hope's tow'ring plumage falls to rise no more!
Of scenes terrestial how the glories fly,
Forget their splendors, and submit to die!
Who ere escap'd thee, but the saint* of old
And the great sage,** whom fiery coursers drew
To heav'n's bright portals from Elisha's view;
Wond'ring he gaz'd at the refulgent car,
Then snatch'd the mantle floating on the air.
From Death these only could exemption boast,
And without dying gain'd th' immortal coast.
Not falling millions sat the tyrant's mind,
Nor can the victor's progress be confin'd.
But cease thy strife with Death, fond Nature, cease:
He leads the virtuous to the realms of peace;
His to conduct to the immortal plains,
Where heav'n's Supreme in bliss and glory reigns.

*Enoch. **Elijah.

106

There sits, illustrious Sir, thy beauteous spouse :
A gem-blaz'd circle beaming on her brows.
Hail'd with acclaim among the heav'nly choirs,
Her soul new-kindling with seraphic fires,
To notes divine she tunes the vocal strings,
While heav'n's high concave with the music rings.
Virtue's rewards can mortal pencil paint ?
No—all descriptive arts, and eloquence are faint ;
Nor canst thou, Oliver, assent refuse
To heav'nly tidings from the Afric muse.

As soon may change thy laws eternal fate,
As the saint miss the glories I relate ;
Or her Benevolence forgotten lie,
Which wip'd the trick'ling tear from Mis'ry's eye.
Whene'er the adverse winds were known to blow,
When loss to loss* ensu'd, and woe to woe,
Calm and serene beneath her father's hand
She sat resign'd to the divine command.

No longer then, great Sir, her death deplore,
And let us hear the mournful sigh no more,
Restrain the sorrow streaming from thine eye,
Be all thy future moments crown'd with joy !
Nor let thy wishes be to earth confin'd,
But soaring high pursue th' unbodied mind.
Forgive the muse, forgive th' advent'rous lays,
That fain thy soul to heav'nly scenes would raise.

*Three amiable Daughters who died when just arrived to Woman's
Estate.

A Farewell to America.

To Mrs. S. W.

I.

Adieu, New-England's smiling meads
Adieu, the flow'ry plain :
I leave thine op'ning charms, O spring
And tempt the roaring main.

II.

In vain for me the flow'rets rise,
And boast their gaudy pride,
·While here beneath the Northern skies
I mourn for health deny'd.

III.

Celestial maid of rosy hue,
O let me feel thy reign !
I languish till thy face I view
Thy vanish'd joys regain.

IV.

Susannah mourns, nor can I bear
To see the crystal flow'r,
Or mark the tender falling tear
At sad departure's hour;

V.

Not unregarding can I see
Her soul with grief opprest
So let no sigh, nor groans for me
Steal from her pensive breast.

VI.

In vain the feather'd warblers sing,
In vain the garden blooms,
And on the bosom of the spring
Breathes out her sweet perfumes.

VII.

While for Britannia's distant shore
We sweep the liquid plain,
And with astonish'd eyes explore
The wide-extended main.

VII.

Lo ! Health appears ! celestial dame !
Complacent and serene,
With Hebe's mantle o'er her Frame,
With soul-deligting mein.

IX.

To mark the vale where London lies
With misty vapors crown'd
Which cloud Aurora's thousand dyes,
And veil her charms around.

X.

Why, Phoebus, moves thy car so slow?
So slow thy rising ray?
Give us the famous town to view,
Thou glorious king of day!

XI.

For thee, Britannia, I resign
New-England's smiling fields;
To view again her charms divine,
What joy the prospect yields!

XII.

But thou! Temptation hence away,
With all thy fatal train
Nor once seduce my soul away,
By thine enchanting strain.

XIII.

Thrice happy they, whose heav'nly shield
Secures their souls from harms
And fell Temptation on the field
Of all its pow'r disarms!

Boston, May 7, 1773.

A Rebus, by J. B.

I.

A bird, delicious to the taste,
On which an an army once did feast,
Sent by an hand unseen;
A creature of the horned race,
Which Britain's royal standards grace;
A gem of vivid green;

II.

A town of gaiety and sport,
Where beaux and beauteous nymphs resort,
And gallantry doth reign;
A Dardan hero fam'd of old
For youth and beauty, as we're told,
And by a monarch slain;

III.

A peer of popular applause,
Who doth our violated laws,
And grievances proclaim.
Th' initials show a vanquished town,
That adds fresh glory and renown
To old Britannia's fame.

111

An Answer to the Rebus, by the Author of These Poems.

The poet asks, and Phillis can't refuse,
To show th' obedience of the Infant muse.
She knows the Quail of most inviting taste
Fed Israel's army in the dreary waste ;
And what's on Britain's royal standard borne,
But the tall, graceful, rampant Unicorn ?
The Emerald with a vivid verdue glows
Among the gems which regal crowns compose ;
Boston's a town, polite and debonair,
To which the beaux and beauteous nymphs repair.
Each Helen strikes the mind with sweet surprise,
While living lightning flashes from her eyes,
See young Euphorbus of the Dardan line
By Menelaus' hand to death resign ;
The well known peer of popular applause
Is G——m zealous to support our laws.
Quebec now vanquish'd must obey,
She too must annual tribute pay
To Britain of immortal fame.
And add new glory to her name.

FINIS